W9-BIN-037

If I Knew Then
What I Know Now...
So What?

If I Knew Then What I Know Now... So What?

ESTELLE GETTY

with Steve Delsohn

CB

CONTEMPORARY
BOOKS

CHICAGO · NEW YORK

Library of Congress Cataloging-in-Publication Data

Getty, Estelle.
    If I knew then what I know now—so what?

    1. Getty, Estelle.   2. Actors—United States—
Biography.   3. Television actors and actresses—United
States—Biography.   I. Delsohn, Steve.   II. Title.
PN2287.G47A3   1988   792'.028'0924 [B]   88-23717
ISBN 0-8092-4474-8

Copyright © 1988 by Estelle Getty and Steve Delsohn
All rights reserved
Published by Contemporary Books, Inc.
180 North Michigan Avenue, Chicago, Illinois 60601
Manufactured in the United States of America
Library of Congress Catalog Card Number: 88-23717
International Standard Book Number: 0-8092-4474-8

Published simultaneously in Canada by Beaverbooks, Ltd.
195 Allstate Parkway, Valleywood Business Park
Markham, Ontario L3R 4T8 Canada

This book is dedicated to my parents,
Sarah and Charles Scher.
You were right; America is indeed the goldena medina—
the golden land of opportunity.
—Estelle Getty

To my parents, Norm and Eilene,
with love.
—Steve Delsohn

Contents

Just So You Know
What You're Getting Into   *11*

1   My Body Was a Temple (Now It's a
Two-Car Garage)   *15*

2   Don't Laugh, Dr. Ruth Would Kill
to Be My Height   *31*

3   "The Golden Girls" (or How a Dazzling
Bombshell like Me Becomes a Little
Old Lady in Twenty Minutes)   *37*

4   Let's Do Lunch:
Surviving Hollywood   *63*

5   Men, Marriage, and Sex (Not Necessarily
in That Order)   *79*

6   Secrets of a Professional Mother   99

7   "So Eat Something":
The Art of Being Jewish   109

8   Confessions of a Hypochondriac   115

9   Do Legends Go to the Bathroom?   129

10   Beyond the Chicken Suit:
Adventures in Theater   139

11   I Get Around:
A Saga of Lost Luggage   155

12   My Fabulous Friends   169

A Last Word . . . or Two   181

If I Knew Then
What I Know Now...
SoWhat?

Just So You Know What You're Getting Into

Me? Writing a book? Maybe next I'll model French bikinis. Who knows? I'm as surprised as anyone else.

I still don't know how all this book stuff happened, but I'll tell you this: be very cautious when you tell people, "Ah, my life, I could write a book." Someone may take you up on it.

I should know. This very nice publisher asked me to write a book, and I said there was one not-so-minor problem: who gives a damn what I have to say?

I also felt a trace of guilt. I know all these wonderful playwrights and aspiring writers who would kill to be published, and suddenly here I come out of deep left field with this book thing. It takes me 50-some years to "make it" as an actress, and suddenly I'm an author in 20 minutes?

But then I figured, why not? My family and friends have heard my shtick for years, and they're still listening. So why not stretch myself? Why not take the risk?

So here I am, writing a book. And I guess I'm a little embarrassed and a little scared and a little shocked, and more than a little delighted.

And also a lot of "What the hell am I doing?"

So here goes. Read and enjoy.

The check is in the mail.
I'll respect you in the morning.
Men are tougher than women.
Uh-huh. Sure.

1
My Body Was a Temple (Now It's a Two-Car Garage)

A wise man—I forget, was it Plato or Ed McMahon?—once said that age is a matter of perspective. It's true. I recently met a woman in the beauty aisle of the supermarket who, I'm delighted to report, had almost as many liver spots as I. We both reached for the Porcelana.

"Don't they drive you crazy?" I asked. "What do you do about them?"

And she said, "What? You mean my beauty marks?"

I thought to myself, *What a lovely point of view.* And so now I regard my liver spots with great affection. I especially adore them in the summer, when they all blend together and I look like I have a very deep tan.

Keeping perspective about your looks is a nice way to keep yourself out of a straitjacket, particularly if you're a woman. Especially out here in Hollywood where every other woman is a ten on a scale of five. Let's face it, in a town that worships the body, mine is sacrilegious.

The fact is, I despise my body. It's fat, it's ugly, it's short, and it has no definition—oh, other than that it's damn hot. Someone once asked me if I ever wished I could trade my body for Cher's. It wouldn't have to be Cher. I would exchange bodies with nine of the first ten people I meet on the street.

And yet these nubile California knockouts actually have the nerve to complain to *me* about *their* looks. I say, "You're a size four and you're nine feet tall, and you're telling me your problems. I really want to hear this—hurry up and finish so I can hit you upside your head."

I laugh about it, but I understand. Every woman, no matter how gorgeous, finds something she hates about her body. Women have it much tougher than men; we're bombarded night and day by the need for physical perfection. You've seen those women who work behind the cosmetics counter at any big department stores? Is there any question that these women were born to (a) work in Bloomingdale's and (b) make the rest of us feel inferior? At 50 they look 22, and have bodies of death. I always comfort myself a little by imagining that their feet must hurt all the time.

I try to be careful: living in Hollywood, you can get all caught up in the age thing. Turning back the clock, looking young, staying fit . . . it's all anyone talks about. Nose jobs, eye jobs, teeth jobs, hair jobs—everyone's getting jobbed. To be honest, I've thought about having my face done. Oh, generally speaking I can get by—I try to go out only at night, when it's dark. And when you make a living pretending to be a woman in her eighties, you're bound to look good by comparison. Still, my wrinkles bother me, not because they make me look old, but because they make my face look sloppy. I would like my face to be neater.

But this quest to be a born-again beauty, especially in California, is almost a cult. And it would be nice if people could give it a rest. I mean, if you're a good person, you're a good person. We all can't be beautiful, tall, thin, and have long, luxurious hair. I'm always relieved when I see a bald guy doing commercials on TV. Bald can be nice too.

I must warn you, however: when it comes to detecting toupees, wigs, whatever, I'm bloodhound. It's not that I try to find fault; to the contrary, if it makes you happy and no one's getting hurt, I say do what you want. Just don't expect to slide one by me. It will never happen.

It all goes back to what I was saying: age, and the

price it extracts from our bodies, is all in your point of view. It's like the time I met this nice young girl who happened to be Miss California.

"My God," I said, "there's something terribly wrong with you."

She looked at me blankly.

"Your whole shape. There's something wrong with your body. You have all this missing flesh on your upper arms. Your stomach goes in instead of out. And your legs, not an inch of crepe."

She said, "Do you have crepe? You look so tiny."

"Darling, I have enough crepe to make a curtain for Radio City Music Hall."

The poor creature went off laughing. Thank God she could smile at her own deformity.

When I was young and my body was (sort of) a temple, no one ever asked me what I thought about old age. Now that my body's a two-car garage, everyone wants to know what I think.

Old age is sneaky. It doesn't come out and say, "Hey, dummy, you're getting old." It's like a leg cramp: it sneaks up on you in the middle of the night.

Even the way you eat takes on new forms. I now need to be fed earlier and earlier. I suppose this is nothing more than a good excuse to squeeze in a few more meals a day—I'm up around five now—but it can also be terribly confusing. Just yesterday I found myself having lunch twice, before breakfast.

When you're young, you can inhale Twinkies during Letterman and sleep like a champ. When you're old, the rules change. Without any provocation, your body will turn on you. And you have no idea why. I mean, if you're 60 years old, and at midnight you consume a pastrami sandwich with Dijon mustard, heartburn is probably what you deserve. But if you've had a piece of dry raisin toast and a cup of herbal tea, and you still get up sick in the morning, you have to ask your stomach, "Hey! What's the problem? Why are you doing this to me?"

So now I try to watch what I eat. And it's hard. Gravity does not take no for an answer. What used to take a week to lose now takes a month. It's hell. Fat is hell.

I'm fatter now than I have been in 40 years. Part of it was leaving New York, where I used to walk all the time. Part of it, no matter where I'm living, is my attitude toward food: if it's the kind that expands the body, I'm all for it. Living in California, where there is no such thing as simple food, hasn't helped a bit. Everything here is incredibly complicated. It's not like New York, where you can walk into a diner and have a scoop of water-packed tuna fish from the can with no mayo and a slice of tomato. Here you order tuna, and it's freshly filleted, char-broiled, served on arugula, drizzled with balsamic vinegar, and covered with capers and the omnipresent avocado.

Though my thighs now need their own condo,

this did not happen overnight. Even as a kid I was fat. As a teenager I lived on grapefruit and black coffee, and I've been dieting ever since. Scarsdale, Stillman—I've failed all of them.

The antidieters aren't much help either. The key to staying thin, they say, is *not* to diet. Eat sensibly, they say. Well, thank you very much, but if I could eat sensibly, why would I have to diet?

The only thing that has changed about my diets is people's reactions when I tell them I'm on one. There was a time when people would say, "You? On a diet? You're such a tiny little thing." Now when I say I'm on a diet, they say, "Uh-huh."

I do what I can. I ride a stationary bike five days a week. On the set, when nothing is happening, I'll stretch and bend on the sidelines. Sometimes I spend the weekend at a spa, which is nice because I have a thing for white terry cloth. I like to keep fit; it makes *me* feel good. Of course, I'll never get as thin as I'd like, so I do the next best thing: I try to hang around with fat people.

* * * * * *

If you're a woman, if you're still breathing, people want to know your age. But they can't fool me. Nobody *really* cares how old you are. All they want to know is whether you look good or rotten for your age. So they can proceed to tell you.

If I told people I was 82, they'd say, "My God, you

look fabulous. How do you do it?" If I told them I was 42, they'd say, "My mother is 60 and looks younger than you." I refuse to cooperate. When people ask me my age, I tell them, "However old you think I am, I look okay for my age."

Why is it that so many people, once they become adults, stop learning? They know what they know—and that's all they *want* to know. If people do things one way for a long enough period of time, they're convinced that automatically makes it right.

I recall the time my mother-in-law, who was in her late sixties, was watching me cook. She was frowning.

"Estelle," she said, "if you put everything in together, you'll save a lot of time."

"That's not the way to do it," I said, "I have to sear the meat first, and then I do the vegetables by themselves."

So we went back and forth until finally she said, "Don't tell me that's not the way to make it. I've been making it that way for 50 years!"

Well, she'd been making it wrong for 50 years.

Our society thinks of age as wisdom. It's not. Experience doesn't give you wisdom. It gives you experience.

I don't necessarily believe or accept what someone says just because he or she is old. Dumb people don't suddenly get smart when they get old, and smart people don't get dumb. If you're dumb when you're young, you'll be dumb when you're old.

Did someone mention sex? No? Well, why not?

I think one of the biggest myths in this country is that old people are not interested in sex. They're very interested, but young people keep telling them they shouldn't be. Old people do have sex, and they have it a lot. They're just doing it a little slower, which, come to think of it, is not a bad thing.

I also don't understand the big taboo about people having sex in retirement homes. I don't get it; it's not like anyone's going to get pregnant. More sex in retirement homes!

Why not? Sex can go on as long as you live and can be just as satisfying when you're 60 as when you're 30. I think "The Golden Girls," in this respect, has been tremendously liberating for America's elderly. There they are on television, older women who aren't afraid to admit they still want, like to talk about, and enjoy having sex. It lets older women say, "Thank God I'm not the only one."

I once did a scene on the show where Sophia is angrily cleaning out her purse, and one of the other girls asks her what she's doing.

"I'm cleaning out my purse," Sophia says with an edge.

"Sophia, why are you so angry?"

"To tell you the truth, I haven't had sex in 15 years, and it's starting to get on my nerves!"

What a wonderful thing for a lady in her eighties to say.

I'm proud to be part of "The Golden Girls"; I think it's a hell of a show. Showing four older women who are willing to experiment with life, to voice their opinions, to say, "I'm part of this society and I can do everything you can do," has done a lot of wonderful things for women my age. Television is a powerful medium, and it's clear from the letters we get that older women now feel freer to express their needs and desires. It's a fulfilling thought.

I also believe wholeheartedly in the concept of Golden Girls—women living communally. Women going to the theater with other women, going to ballparks and taking cruises with other women, and having a perfectly lovely time.

I've always felt that loneliness, not age, is the real killer. I get a lot of letters from women who tell me how difficult life is—they're widowed and alone and scared and sick—and the show cheers them up. And how they'd love to be like Sophia and live with other women—but they don't. They've lost their husbands; now they feel bereft of all peace and security.

Letters like that always move me, because it doesn't have to be that way. It all goes back to the Noah's Ark syndrome which prevails in our society, the notion that people have to go through life two by two. That you're less than whole—this goes for men and women and gays of both sexes.

Damn it, it isn't so. Divorce, widowhood, break-ups—they make all of us hurt. But life doesn't end, and life can be perfectly viable for a single person. It takes courage to reach out and form new relation-ships. But that courage has great rewards.

* * * * * *

I confess. I can no longer remember names.

Fortunately, it doesn't matter. I can have entire conversations with friends and my sister by the hour, in which none of us will mention a name, yet we all know exactly what, and whom we're discuss-ing.

"Remember the actor who used to always play the bad guy?"

"With the cleft in his chin?"

"Right, well he's dating that woman who almost went to jail for embezzlement."

"Yeah? I thought he was dating the actress who was in that movie where they take away the baby because she's an unfit mother and then the tall guy, the one from *The Three Musketeers*, comes along and gets the kid back."

"They broke up. She married the singer with the terrible toupee."

See? It's easy.

Memory erosion: it's a fact of age. But losing things—that's another matter. If you're a loser, you're a loser, whether you're 5 or 85, although I lose fewer things now than I did when I was younger. I used to leave my mother's house, and she'd say to me, "Now hold on to your umbrella and your gloves and tie your scarf around your neck and keep your hat on your head—otherwise you'll lose them." And I was married at the time.

Keys, forget about it. I'm notorious, even now. My son, Carl, once gave me a keychain that supposedly you couldn't lose: if you clapped three times, it made this little whine. The thing never worked: I'd walk around the house applauding, and that keychain couldn't care less. It only worked when I was in the car, and only then at specific moments: the minute I'd get lost or nervous, the thing would beep like crazy. I had to keep it, though; not only was it a gift from my son, but I was convinced the damn thing had a soul of its own.

I make a lot of jokes about age, and I do it for a reason: it ain't going away.

I have this theory about aging: the best way to hold it at bay is to make it your friend instead of your nemesis. Keep on doing whatever it is you've been doing. Do it as long as you can, even if you have to force yourself to do it. Once you stop doing, you simply forget how to start again.

If you live long enough, thank God, you're *going* to get old. And no matter how many face lifts you have, gravity will eventually overpower you and there will be nothing left to lift. I'm not saying that you have to embrace old age, but we've got to stop fighting the idea that we can cling to our youth forever. You've got to say, okay, I'll stay as well as I can, I'll do my thing, but I'm not going to sit around and mourn my youth. *That* will make you old.

As you might guess, I'm not big on retirement. I'm going to work until I drop, and maybe then too. I do know some people who love their retirement—they can play all the golf and catch all the fish and plant all the flowers and listen to all the music they never had time for. It's definitely an individual thing.

But if I had to make comparisons, I'd say this is much more common: the first few weeks of retirement are great. Then they have golf balls and fish coming out their ears. You see these men who used to have professions, jobs, businesses, and responsibilities, and now they're lost souls. Every two minutes they poke their heads into the kitchen and ask their poor wives, "Should I go and buy bananas?"

How do you know when you're *really* getting older?

When you give advice 25 hours a day, solicited or not. You tell people what to eat, what to drink, what to name their fish. And you start to give very specific instructions. "Lick the stamp first. *Then* put it on the envelope."

I do this to my friend David. I had the foresight to warn him: "Every time I start to do it, tell me I'm doing it." He tells me, "Estelle, you're doing it," but apparently it isn't working. When David dies, he says his tombstone will bear a simple message: *Here Lies J. David Krassner. Estelle Was Right.*

Okay, so I give a lot of instructions—over and over again. Older people tend to do this a lot, especially to young people. You give the same instruction several times because you *know* that the person you're telling is much too young, too busy, and too glamorous to possibly remember something so "old" and mundane.

Or maybe it's something else: maybe it's to assure yourself. Yes, to assure yourself that you can still remember things. If you say things out loud several times—don't forget to turn off the lights and pick up the mail and turn off the water—it might make you feel better: "Hey, I might be old, but I sure as hell can remember things."

One thing age hasn't hampered is my ability to drive. I drive fine, although I'm still relatively inept when it comes to directions. I get lost getting out of my pajamas.

Young people love to complain about older drivers, but they're not alone. Old people also love to complain about older drivers. It's a matter of perspective. When the other guy makes a mistake, it's because he's too old to be driving: "That old nipplehead, that old dodo, that old pea brain, they should take away his license!" When *you* run five cars off the road, it's "Oh, I made a mistake. So kill me."

Old pea brain drivers are bad enough. But there's a particular species you must avoid at all costs, and I'll tell you the same thing I've always told my husband, Arthur: never drive behind a man who wears a hat in the car. Guaranteed, there's something amiss when a man feels compelled to wear his hat in the car. Change lanes immediately.

You Know You're Getting Old When . . .

- Someone tells you he's moving to the country in May, and you say, "So, when are you moving to the country?"
- You eat a caramel and lose a filling.
- You pet a dog and lose a filling.
- You move your bed closer to the bathroom because you spend half the night there anyway.
- No matter what time you go to bed, eight in the evening or three in the morning, you wake up at the exact same time.
- You think you're running and you're not.
- No matter how formal the outing, you still wear low-heeled shoes.
- No matter how annoyed you used to get when your mother was constantly on the lookout for steps, you find yourself asking every two minutes, "Is that a step?"
- In the dictionary under "Allergic" there's a picture of you.

- At a boring party, you used to nod and smile and say to yourself, I should leave, this is boring. Now you jump up and shout, "I'm leaving! This is boring!"
- You only like people who think exactly as you do.
- You leave the kitchen, go into the living room, forget what you went into the living room for, go back into the kitchen so you'll remember what you wanted, remember it's time to eat, make yourself a turkey sandwich, and forget that you ever left the kitchen in the first place.
- You tend to repeat yourself.
- No one gives you perfume. Your entire house is filled instead with little *tchatchkes*—vases and little boxes and paperweights and picture frames and other little trinkets that people give you because they don't know what else to give you because they think you're old and you already have everything.
- Your most treasured possession, next to your glasses, is your backup pair of glasses.
- You take other people's stories and make them your own—and you believe yourself.
- You tend to repeat yourself.
- You welcome fat because it fills out the wrinkles.
- You tend to repeat yourself.

You know the tags that say "One Size Fits All"? I'd like to take a big red pen and write "Like Hell!" on every one of those tags.

2
Don't Laugh,
Dr. Ruth Would Kill
to Be My Height

I am short. I have always been short. Chances are,
I will get shorter.

In my early days as an actress hungry for parts, I
utilized every trick imaginable to hide my limited
stature. I would enter an audition, and if the director stood to greet me, I would quickly sit down so
he wouldn't notice my limited stature. When I went to
leave, I would rush to stand before he did. When I
would audition with other people, even normal-
sized people, I would stand as far away as possible; if
the actor was uncommonly tall, I would stand just
outside of New Jersey. If he moved closer, I would

tell him, "Please, I need my space."

Though I am under five feet tall, it is of no great wonder to me. My family is small, so it doesn't shock me that I should be small.

So why does it astonish everyone else?

I am a lady well into my years. It's apparent, I like to think, that I possess at least normal intelligence. I pride myself on being self-aware. So what I find hard to comprehend is this: why are people so compelled to look at me and say to themselves, "She's very short. I *must* call this to her attention." If someone has lived a lifetime with a birthmark on his cheek, you're something less than a rocket scientist if you need to point out to him, "You have a large red birthmark on your cheek." Isn't it fair to assume, if that person has a minimum-to-average-sized brain, at some point he's noticed it?

Yet people never get over the wonder of my smallness. There are three types. Those of the first type call it to my attention as though it was *their* discovery. "You know, you're very small," they pronounce.

And I say, "No! My God! Are you serious?!" Then I run to a mirror and say, "My goodness, you're absolutely right! Thank you for pointing that out. I had no idea."

Then there are people who *accuse* me of being small. In a stern voice they say, "You are short. You are very short. I had no idea you were this short."

And I say, "I'm sorry. I hope I didn't offend you.

The fact of the matter is, I was given the choice to be five-foot-eight, but I was young at the time, very, very young, and I stupidly said, 'No, I want to be under five feet.' Now I realize this was a grave mistake."

Finally there are people who grant me *permission* to be short. They say, "It's okay. My aunt Rose was your size." As if now, by knowing that Aunt Rose, the aunt of this person I've never met, is short, I can find the strength to continue my life. Now I can better accept my plight.

It never relents. Recently I was approached by a newspaper reporter. First she looked me over. Then she began to shake her head, sympathetically, as she might at a cow with three legs.

"I never realized you were this short," she finally said.

I said, "Well, come to the realization right now. Can you live with it? Can you take it? Can you bear it?"

She said, "My God, you're the smallest person I ever saw."

I said, "Well, I guess that makes me the winner."

Finally she asked me, "So. How tall are you are?"

I said, "None of your business."

Being short is no day at Neiman-Marcus. In this country it is the last bastion of prejudice (yes, really). If a tall person and a short person apply for the same job, the tall person will get it, unless the job involves sitting on a racehorse. Tall people also make more money than short people. My feeling is, when you're short you have to work harder. In more ways than one, you have no stature.

You know the tags that say "One Size Fits All"? I'd like to take a big red pen and write "Like Hell!" on every one of those tags.

One size fits all *what*?

Certainly not this kid. One size fits people who are five-foot-five and weigh 135 pounds and have shoulders like Willard Scott. One size does not fit all. "One Size" does not even fit petites, and a petite is someone who's five-foot-three. My *fantasy* is to be five-foot-three.

Thank God for purses and shoes. I love them— they're the only two things in my life that I don't have to have altered. So I've got purses and shoes up the wazoo. Betty White keeps a running count to see how long I can arrive on the set without repeating a pair of shoes.

Fact: there is no such thing as clothes that fit me. Fact: my friends refuse to believe this. They keep saying, "Ah, come on, I could take you places where they can fit you." And I tell them, "No, no you can't." But they'll insist, and because I love them, I'll go along to their stores. Hours of failures later, they reluctantly concede that I was right. Maybe they think because I'm old I'm not hip to the newest places. I am hip. I'm also short.

For a long time I bought clothes in the children's

department. Then, as I reached a certain age and the clothes for kids got crazier, I had to stop. From that day on it was Alteration City. All of which delighted my tailor, who is now buying a home on Rodeo Drive.

Not that my frustration has stopped me from buying clothes. What kind of wimp do you think I am? I have five full closets. I confess . . . I'm a clothes pony.

But as small as I may be, God has been good—at least he made a few people smaller than I. I was once asked to MC an event for the Writers Guild, along with Bea Arthur and Rue McClanahan and Betty White. But as I neared the stage I suddenly realized there was no way I could see over the podium. So in the middle of the show, I told the gentleman who was introducing me that I needed a little step. Meanwhile, the audience is listening and laughing and everyone is running around backstage looking for a step. Finally they brought out the step. I climbed up, peered over the podium, and the audience, still laughing, broke into applause.

"You can laugh all you want," I said. "Dr. Ruth would kill to be this height."

You never know what's going to happen on our set. You'll have to read something, a note or a letter, and instead of the note you're expecting there'll be an obscene poem. Or you'll open the refrigerator and there will be a rubber snake. Or a cobweb. Or something will leap out at you from the freezer.

3
"The Golden Girls" (or How a Dazzling Bombshell like Me Becomes a Little Old Lady in Twenty Minutes)

I'm mad, crazy, insanely in love with Woody Allen. The man should be made a prince, a president, coach of his beloved New York Knicks. Anything he wants, give it to him, tax-free.

Mister Allen tells a wonderful story. He was drowning, going down for the third and final time, and suddenly his life began to flash before his eyes. He saw a picture of this little towheaded boy walking through the fields of Iowa with a fishing pole, going to town to buy Emmy Lou a piece of gingham so she could make herself a new frock—when he realized the wrong life was flashing before his eyes. He was from Brooklyn.

I can relate. It's the same way I feel about "The Golden Girls."

After all those years of paying more dues than the Teamsters, after all those small, off-off-Broadway, off-Broadway, and finally Broadway theaters, suddenly I'm this so-called "celebrity." I'm one of the "stars" of one of the top five rated shows on television.

I wish I were sophisticated enough to tell you that all of this is nothing less than I expected. The truth is, it's astonishing. "The Golden Girls"—all of it—exceeds my craziest dreams.

And that's why I feel like that Woody Allen bit, like I'm living someone else's life. I'm quite sure that all this good fortune was meant for someone else, and any day that person will tap me on the shoulder and say, "Hey, shorty, you're living my life. Get lost!"

Before "The Golden Girls," Hollywood was neither my dream nor my ambition. I was thrilled and content to work in the New York theater. It was there, during my five-year stint in the Broadway hit *Torch Song Trilogy*, that I was finally getting some recognition.

But as *Torch Song* got hotter, the people I knew began to talk. Go west, they said; go to Hollywood. And I'd laugh and say, Of course, Hollywood awaits me with baited breath so it can finally get off the ground.

The only reason I tried Hollywood in 1985 was to

put to rest the notion that I could "make it" there. Then I could die contentedly, saying, "See? It was never meant to be."

Then—hello, new life—"The Golden Girls" came along.

Actually, I had been to Hollywood about a year or so before with the West Coast swing of *Torch Song*, and during that time I had done a few soaps, a few small parts in movies, some TV things, but nothing that had garnered much notice. Now I was returning, not as one of the stars of *Torch Song*, but as Estelle Getty. Period. I told my managers, Alan Siegel and Juliet Green, "two months." If nothing happens, and I was willing to bet it wouldn't, I was going back east.

Six weeks later I was Sophia.

It was kind of a fluke. When I read the pilot, I said, "Yes, this is a nice part. I think I can do a good job." And my agent said, "Hey, that's the role of Dorothy [the part that went to Bea Arthur]." I, he explained, was reading for the part of Sophia.

"But that's an old lady!" I protested.

Not just old, but 80. Not just 80, but rotund and Italian with hair worn in a bun. Fat I knew I could handle; fat I was good at. Rotund might take a few weeks.

As for playing 80 and Italian, I'd certainly played age and ethnic before. Still, given the part as a whole, and my congenital inclination to expect the worst, I had more than my share of doubts.

My agent, Harris/Goldberg, like any good agent, suggested I go in and see what I could do, and like any good actress I did. But first I made a decision with the help of my friend, writer Joel Kimmel, who advised me to "do what you do best, make 'em laugh": I would play Sophia my way. I would play her New York Brooklyn.

When I read for the part, the producers seemed pleased, but there was also a reservation: they thought I might be too young (please, no cracks). I was called back to read again . . . and again . . . and again . . . and again. I had never auditioned that many times for one role. Typically you go in, get one callback, two at the most, and either you get the part or you don't. This time the process took over a month.

Each time they told my agents, "Tell her not to change anything; tell her to do exactly the same thing." I kept wondering, *if they don't want me to change anything, then why do they keep asking me back?*

I was in a quandary when, just before my final audition, we had a brilliant inspiration: I would *dress* as a little old lady! I drove to a thrift shop, bought a size 12 checked polyester dress, lace-up orthopedic shoes, a straw hat with a veil, a pocketbook, and gloves. I whitened my hair and had a makeup man come to my house to make me look old. And it was dressed like this, embarrassed down to my little-old-lady socks, that I walked through the corridors of NBC to read one last time for the part of Sophia.

When I entered the room for my reading, it was Big Shot City. Brandon Tartikoff, the top man at NBC, Susan Harris, the show's creator, and several other network heavyweights sat waiting. I read, the same way I had the other three times. When I was finished they applauded, which doesn't happen very often, and I thought that was sweet.

The casting agent approached: could I wait for twenty minutes? My mind began to race. *What does it mean? Am I in, am I out, do they love me, do they hate me, if a tree falls in the forest and no one hears it, does it make a noise?*

But I responded coolly, "Yes, of course."

The next 20 minutes passed as quickly as the Ice Age. Then the casting agent reappeared.

"Thank you," she said. "Thank you very much. You can leave now."

Ouch.

And that, I figured, was that. I walked out to the lot with Alan and got back in the car. "Honey," I said to him, "we almost made it. We really did. We were *that* close."

Once I got home, all alone, I felt like a tire someone had deflated. It's the crazy thing about being an actor: there is no second place. You can be one breath from the biggest role of your life, and if you don't get it, you don't get it the same way the guy riding the subway doesn't get it.

On the other hand, I'm a pessimist . . . I really hadn't expected to get it anyway . . . no one comes to Hollywood and lands a series in two months . . . it's preposterous . . . I'm not that kind of dreamer . . . who was I kidding? Who *was* I kidding? I wanted that part.

That evening I had to work. I was doing a TV movie, *Copacabana*, with Barry Manilow, a dear, sweet man whom I love. Barry had somehow managed to cheer me up, when I was told I had a message to call my managers. I started to hope . . . no, it couldn't be. I called them back.

They both started screaming, *"You got it! You got it! You got it!"*

It's kind of a blur, but I think I threw up my hands, like people do on game shows when they win a lot of furniture, and screamed out "YEEEOOWWW!!"

And then reality set in.

Can I do it? Have they made a mistake? What if I get a cold sore?

That was me, my first day on the job. Outwardly I was calm and professional. Inside my stomach was doing the rumba.

As usual I was early, the first one to arrive. And then in walks Bea Arthur. And I thought, *Oh my God, that's Bea Arthur, and we're going to be*

*working together, I'm going to play her mother,
Oh my God.* And then Betty White walked in and I
thought, *Look at her—she's just like she is on TV,
bubbly and sweet and perfect. Look at her, look at
her.* And then Rue McClanahan walked in and I
thought, *I've always loved her on the stage—she's
so truly talented and so lovely. Oh my God, oh my
God.*

Intimidated? Like Custer. I couldn't help myself.
I'd never felt that way around the theater, but this
was TELEVISION and these women were giants in
the business. I remember fretting silently, what if
they think I stink?

We did the first show, and mercifully it seemed to
go all right. After it was over Bea Arthur approached me. She put her arm around me and gave
me a kiss.

"You're terrific," she said, smiling down at me.

I was purely thrilled; here was Bea Arthur, this
legend, validating my work in a medium to which I
was mostly a stranger. It was the beginning of a
beautiful relationship.

Not just for Bea and me, but for all of us. These
three women—and I don't say this because it
sounds nice, I say this because I mean it with all my
heart—took me along for what has been a hell of a
ride. They just swept me along with all their talent.
I'm sure they could have done the same for anyone
with a modicum of skill.

Their generosity was remarkable. I was amazed

the first time Bea said, "That's not really a line for me; I think that's a line for Estelle. That should be a Sophia line." Or Rue said, "I can't stand here, Estelle's face is in the shadow." Or Betty said, "When you're talking to me at the door, see that the door is behind your shoulder; otherwise there's going to be a shadow on your face." I haven't been in television long, but I know that this type of caring is unheard of.

So if you're looking to hear about feuds, I can't help you. I'm told there are shows in which the stars count lines and complain if someone is getting too many. Or, "How come she's doing that scene and I'm not even in it?" On our show, forget it—I have never heard *one* remark to that effect. Not only have we never had a single fight, but among us there exists a totally genuine respect and regard and caring. And I'm not saying that because I'm writing a book. If it wasn't true, I would just leave it out.

As much as we care about each other, though, the tabloids would have you think we engage in daily fistfights. It's nothing like a "Dallas" or a "Dynasty"—tabloid heaven—but "The Golden Girls" does get its share of invented stories. The tabloids go out of their way to be outrageous: they would love for you to sue because all that does is increase their circulation tenfold. So I simply forget it and let it go.

But the first time it happened I was wildly distressed. They said some insane, nasty things about me, that I was fighting with the writers and had threatened to quit and was demanding a $5,000-a-week raise. I was shocked when I heard about the "story," and I called one of the producers.

"It's not true," I said.

"What's not?" he said.

"What's written in the paper."

"Which paper?"

I told him.

"Oh," he said. "I've got to go get it."

I said, "You mean you didn't read it?"

"No."

"So why did I open my big mouth?"

He laughed, and that was the end of it. I quickly learned not to pay those papers any mind—no one in the business does. My only advice to people who do read them is not to believe a single word.

So, yes, the women on the show all get along, though it's not because we have much in common. Our backgrounds are so diverse it's as if we're from four different corners of the earth. Bea is from New York but grew up in a small town in Maryland; when she was younger, she dreamed of and realized a career as a singer and actress. Rue lived in Oklahoma, where her father was in construction, her mother owned a beauty parlor, and she was a dancer from the time she was a little girl. Betty's a native Californian, the adored only child of a family that was totally WASP. And I'm this first-generation American from the lower east side of Manhattan.

Yet here we are, thrown together with a common goal, and despite our differences the chemistry works. Part of that has nothing to do with show business: the women I work with are simply wonderful human beings. But they're also ultimate professionals: no one actress feels she's bigger than the show. It's "The Golden Girls," always, that matters to us most.

It's much easier to have this attitude when all the written roles are meaty and real, as ours are. It also leads to the inevitable question: how much do the actors and their characters have in common? I'll talk about Sophia and me in a moment, but as for the other women—NO! They're not like their characters at all.

Take Bea, for example. What she has in common with Dorothy is that she is certainly as funny and witty. Conversely, not as abrasive or tough as the Emmy-winning Maude she played for so many years. The real Bea is as tough as rice cakes. She's shy, sensitive, tender, extremely private—and more fragile than you might expect.

Bea is not "Hollywood." The last thing you ever want to do is slobber and fawn all over her. That first day on the set when Bea walked in, I walked up and told her what a fan I was. She smiled and simply nodded. I got the message: Bea is sweet but doesn't like you to make a fuss.

She'd rather spend three days in solitary confinement than three hours doing a public appearance.

She's extremely bright and has plenty to say, but she has little patience for publicity events. But as much as Bea dislikes PR and photo sessions, she winds up doing them anyway just like the rest of us. And then because of her they always run long: she's so funny we can't get anything done. When Bea is being funny, which is often, she's so funny you could die. And no one tells a better naughty joke than Bea Arthur.

I've been asked many times when I realized that "The Golden Girls" would be a hit. It was when I heard that Bea Arthur was going to be in it. I couldn't imagine her committing to anything that would *not* be a hit. Of course, whenever she hears me say that, Bea laughs and insists it isn't so.

But it is.

There were two other ingredients that made me sure the show would be a hit: Betty White and Rue McClanahan.

The whole country's in love with Betty White; the minute you meet her you know why. She's the All-American ideal. Betty's open, gentle, loving, and talks to every person as if he or she is the most important soul on this earth.

Betty makes jokes about how long she's been around, how she got her start in silent TV. Take my word for it—I see her every day—this is a woman who does not age. The first thing you notice about Betty is her beauty. Not TV beautiful, not fadingly beautiful. She's simply *beautiful*, like she always has been.

I have no idea how Betty manages always to look so fresh, because she never stops working. She works Saturdays, Sundays, holidays, weekends— amazingly, she's constantly upbeat. No one works harder and makes it seem more effortless.

Betty's also extremely daring: if someone asked her to ride a unicycle, I'm sure she'd give it a shot. She lives her life with zest . . . especially when it involves animals. I'm convinced Betty could tell a charging lion, "Come here, pussycat, sit on my lap," and the lion would join her for Oreos and milk. Betty's love for animals is legendary—and well deserved.

Unlike her character, Rose, Betty is extremely intelligent. *Like* Rose, Betty's goal in life is for everything to be nice. If you step on her toe, she will apologize to you.

Betty White is Miss America.

Rue McClanahan is a doer. Life excites her. Cross-country skiing, a new diet—Rue will be the first to jump right in. Tell Rue you know a person who went 40,000 feet below the sea, or climbed Everest, and she'll say, "Oh, I'd like to do that. That sounds so interesting." She sews, embroiders, writes music and plays, acts, and dances. She also plants fruit trees, picks the fruit, and cans it herself. Excuse me, I think I'll go lie down now.

Rue tells these wonderful stories about her hometown in Oklahoma, where everybody has two or three names, like Billy Bob or Jimmy Joe Ray, and that's just the women. Every so often a "whizbang" or a "whizdooly" will slip into Rue's conversation. I have no idea what she means, but I love to hear her say it.

We kid Rue a lot about her catnaps. She can sleep anyplace, anytime, for 15 minutes or 15 hours. I always tell her, "You must have the clearest conscience on earth." Give Rue five minutes and she'll take Rip Van Winkle.

One time we lost her. We took a five-minute break and when the five minutes were up, no Rue. We searched the dressing room, her car, the ladies' room, all over the lot. We were pacing, calling— she'd simply disappeared.

We were getting concerned when finally somebody walked behind the couch on the set and there was Rue—fast asleep—lying on the floor. She didn't want to be disturbed by the glare of the light on the couch, so she'd gone behind it. We roared.

Like Bea and Betty, Rue is what I call a total animal nut. I can't keep track of their animals: Is Earl the cat or the dog? Is Leo the bird or the fish? I'm a supporter of animal rights too, but not to the extent of the other ladies. Once I arrived at an awards ceremony wearing a fox jacket. It wasn't even mine; I had borrowed it from a friend for the night. Bea wouldn't even let me sit at the table. She shouted at me and told me to get away from the table while I was wearing that fox.

The other women won't even trap mice in their attic unless it's done humanely. Rue told me a cat once brought her a rodent—I think it was a field mouse—and dropped it at her feet. It wasn't dead yet, so she nursed it back to health and took it to the vet.

"Are you out of your mind?" I said. "What did you think was going to happen? That it would go out, get a job, and make a living for you out of gratitude?"

Rue always laughs when I mention this and categorically insists I made it up. Personally, I'm sure that story's perfectly true.

Rue plays Blanche on the show, our resident man trap. Blanche talks a much bigger game than she plays, but this hasn't stopped Rue's father from objecting to some of her saltier lines. He'll call and tell her, "You've gone a little too far this time, Missy."

Rue's father isn't alone; other people have said the show features too much talk of sex. I don't agree, but I can appreciate their feelings—it all depends on your perspective. I can tell you many more people like the show than don't, because it's popular not only here, but in Scotland, Australia, New Zealand, Spain . . . something like 27 different countries. My personal feeling is that if it isn't racy or demeaning to women, I have no problem with it.

And I don't think we're any of those things.

Rue, as I said, is nothing like Blanche. She likes men all right, but not like Blanche. (Does *anyone* like men as much as Blanche?) But this hasn't deterred her many male fans. Men are crazy about Rue . . . including one I know quite well.

On the walls of my husband's office in Miami, Arthur has hung up some pictures of me. Once a customer came in and asked him what's with all the pictures. Arthur explained that I was his wife.

The customer looked at him funny. "Estelle Getty is your wife?"

"Yes," Arthur said.

"From 'The Golden Girls'?"

"Yes, from 'The Golden Girls.' "

"I don't believe it."

"Why should I lie?" Arthur said. "If I was going to lie, I'd put up pictures of Rue McClanahan."

People love to hear what goes on behind the scenes, and on our show there's plenty to tell about. But first, a warning:

If you've got a bad toupee, stay away from Bea Arthur.

It's not that Bea objects to toupees. It's just that when she sees a bad one, one that's a trifle too blatant, she can't keep a straight face. We once had a guest on the show, a man none of us had previously met, and when he arrived on the set the poor man was wearing this toupee that stood so far up in front you could see his scalp. When I introduced him to Bea, she turned to say hello and, without benefit of advance warning, was quickly reduced to hysterical laughter.

I was ready for this.

"Oh, she's so impossible," I explained. "The minute she sees me she starts to laugh. It doesn't even matter what I say. She just laughs."

This went on all day. And every time Bea would break up, I'd look at her, shake my head, and say, "That Bea. I just crack her up."

When Bea starts to laugh, it's like a dam breaking. She can't stop. Her laugh is all her own: the face will flush, the hands will flail, the tears will begin to cascade down her cheeks, but you won't hear a sound. She'll go on and on like this, silently, and then *everyone* will be hysterical. Sometimes we don't even know what we're laughing about. One afternoon the producers made us take a break because we couldn't stop laughing. We felt like kids in study hall.

We had one episode where Sophia was winning an award. The lady hosting the awards show says, "Don Johnson was supposed to be here, but he couldn't make it. His producers, however, have sent over his clothes." She goes backstage and returns with a pair of white pants and a pastel jacket with rolled up sleeves. Well, this tickled Bea to the point of hysteria. Each time they would bring out Don Johnson's clothes, Bea would totally break up and couldn't go on with the scene. None of us, for fear of losing it too, could even glance at her. It's funny even now if you see the rerun: even when the lines are directed at Bea, no one is looking at her.

Staying loose, for us, has never been a problem. We tell each other jokes, unusual stories, intimacies from our very different lives. And there's a lot of bawdy humor.

Except on Thursday and Friday. We made a mortifying discovery: on Thursday and Friday the mikes are open. Every word we say is broadcast throughout the offices of everyone involved in the show. That can be pretty embarrassing, so now, whenever one of us begins to say something personal or naughty, we point to the mike and remind ourselves to whisper.

While I'm on the topic of comic relief, I should mention our two prop men, Ken and Jimmy. Ken and Jimmy are excellent, dedicated prop men who take great pride in their work.

They are also certifiably insane. There is nothing they won't do, no level they won't stoop to, to execute a practical joke. If it takes all night to set up a gag, they will do it. Jokes, for them, are no joke.

We had one episode where Blanche is giving out Christmas presents. They're homemade calendars, with pictures of her many different boyfriends, one for each month of the year. Blanche being Blanche, the poses are rather risqué. The way the scene goes, Bea opens to one of the months and whistles.

"Which one?" I ask.

"September," Bea answers.

I leaf quickly to September and then look at Blanche. "This is September? It's a wonder you could walk in October."

Naturally, we were using regular calendars in rehearsal all week (the audience would never know). But at the actual taping, we took out the calendars, flipped them open—and realized our prop men had deep psychiatric problems. Ken and Jimmy had stayed up all night taking nude and seminude pictures of each other, in all manner of riotous poses. The entire cast was hysterical in tears.

I could go on forever . . . the time I went to pick up my suitcase and they had filled it with bricks . . . the time they nailed Herb Edelman's lunchbox to a stool . . . the time Rue was embroidering a large, beautiful bedspread, came back from a break to find an ice cream cone melted right on top of it, screamed, "Oh my God, who did this?" and discovered it was rubber.

Ken and Jimmy are also very big on shock, especially mid-scene. We'll have to read something, a note or a letter, and instead of the note we're expecting there'll be an obscene little poem from Ken and Jim. Or we'll open the refrigerator and there will be a rubber snake. Or a cobweb. Or something will leap out of the freezer.

The audience is never safe either. Friday evening,

the night we tape the show, the tension will build, the audience will get excited, the cast will be getting pumped up for the big event. Suddenly Ken and Jimmy, in full view of cast and crowd, will start to argue. Ken will push Jimmy, Jimmy will push Ken. Jimmy will rip Ken's shirt, Ken will rip Jimmy's shirt. Ken will pull at Jimmy's belt—Jimmy's pants will fall. And he'll be wearing women's panties.

Welcome to the urbane world of network TV.

* * * * * *

"Who needs this aggravation? Who needs show business? I should retire and go live down in Florida in a condominium like my sister Roz."

Those rantings are mine, administered to Rue and Betty and Bea every Friday night, the night we tape the show, a time when normal people are loosening up, eagerly beginning their weekends. And I'm searching for a tall bridge from which to dive off.

Do I have stage fright? No, my hair always looks like Don King's.

The other women don't have stage fright. Oh, they may show a trace now and then, but it pales by comparison to me. Every Friday night, 26 weeks a year, I feel like I've swallowed a sock.

I've tried everything, even hypnosis, and I can't whip it. So every Friday night I do a lot of silent hoping and praying. "Get me through this and I'll be a better person, I'll do more charity, I'll lay off the Snickers. *Please.* Just get me through this."

The terror I feel is the most difficult thing I've ever had to face. Facts like this don't help: the first time I was on television doing "The Golden Girls," more people saw me that *one* night than in my entire 50-year career.

Picture it—as Sophia is wont to say.

The theater was different: there I was secure. In the theater you go out with a polished project that's been rehearsed for many weeks. TV, which I find infinitely more difficult, is like the freeway at rush hour. Lines get rewritten all week—you learn and unlearn and relearn. You must do the script verbatim, and do it and do it and do it, until you get it perfect. When I make a mistake during a taping, the studio audience sees me, and I find that terribly embarrassing. On the nights when the tapings run long, it's usually because I've held us up.

Anybody know a good realtor in Miami?

* * * * * *

The show is now entering its fourth year, and people know who I am. The first year was much different. I was doing little publicity, and when people would meet me, they'd be flabbergasted to learn that I was the actress who played Sophia. After they retrieved their jaws, the first thing they'd always say was "How long does it take to make you into Sophia?"

I wish I could have said 4 hours. The truth is, it's more like 45 minutes.

There are two reasons for this: Maurice Stein, our makeup man, is marvelous, one of the best in the business. He also has the easiest job in the world. All those lines in Sophia's neck are really mine—Maurice doesn't have to *create* anything. He just fills in the lines that are already there.

Originally the makeup people were planning on using latex, which is like liquid rubber glued to the skin. Instead they decided to use several layers of makeup, done completely with shadows and lines and pencils. It's a tricky process, and helpful person that I am, I tried to relax Maurice.

I told him, "Look, to you this is just another job. But this is my life. Screw this up and I'm ruined . . . but I don't want to put any pressure on you."

There are times when Maurice is finished and I look in the mirror and think I don't look old enough. Other times I tell him, "You made me look 95. I look like a scarecrow." He'll say, "I'm sorry. It's not my fault. I work with what I have."

One of these days, Maurice. . . .

At some point the kidding will stop; we'll both get very quiet. For me this time is critical: it's not until this point, this last half hour before we tape, that I *become* Sophia. People on the street always say to me, "Say something like Sophia." I can't. Sophia doesn't breathe until I get on the makeup and the wig.

To me it's my job. To others it must look strange. I'm from New York. I have lived my life in fast forward. I walk fast, talk fast, eat faster than anyone I know. So-I-rush-into-the-chair-as-Estelle . . . and . . . by . . . the . . . time . . . I . . . slowly . . . climb . . . out . . . I'm . . . Sophia.

It just seems to happen that way. I look in the mirror and see an old lady. And I become this old lady.

I'm used to it now, but the first time was a shock. I stood up, I looked in the mirror—my hair was white, my shoulders were slumped, my eyes looked old—and I thought, *Oh my God, is that really you?*

But once it's over, it's over. The minute I take off the wig and the makeup I'm back to me. The minute I walk out the door my life speeds back up. I've never understood actors who have to go to tremendous psychological pains to exit their character. I get into it quickly, I get out of it quickly. I feel it's the only way. Otherwise I'd go through life bogged down with the baggage of characters I've played for 50 years.

No, thank you, I'm neurotic enough as it is.

As a student of human nature, I love to people-watch. It's also essential to my craft—I'll pick things up I see on the street and incorporate them into my roles. It was my idea, for instance, for Sophia and her handbag to never be parted. Not that she carries one, but that she never puts it down.

Elderly women, and I've seen this a hundred times, never put their purses down. I think I know why: when you displace people, take them from the homes they've had for 40, 50, 60 years, when you take their furniture and their dishes and their pots and their pans, and you put them in some retire-ment home, or even in the home of their children, you take away everything that's familiar. What they have left—the things they hold precious—go in their purses: the medicine, personal treasures, pic-tures of the grandchildren, important cards and documents. Putting down your purse is like putting down your life.

I went to England a few years ago, and while I was there I checked out my theory. I was right. Have you ever seen the queen without *her* purse?

I can enter a room or walk through a mall, and absolute strangers will run up, kiss me, hug me, and twirl me in the air, shouting, "I love you! I really love you!" I'll be thinking, *How do I know these people?* And they'll say, "We're from Canada! We watch your show every Saturday night, and we love you!"

Does it bother me?

It's the greatest!

I can't tell you how tremendously satisfying it is to be the object of all that love. How many accoun-tants, how many bricklayers, how many dentists, how many electricians are told "I love you" every day of their lives by people they meet? It's incredi-ble. And when people ask me, "Was it worth it all those years?" my answer is "Absolutely!"

But I'm also no fool. I realize total strangers don't know Estelle. They know—and love—Sophia.

Oh, I'm sure there are a lot of older people who identify with *me*, who are delighted that somebody their age, one of their own, has made it after all these years. I'm sure there's a burst of pride: "See, she's old like me, but she's still going strong!" Everyone likes to see a peer succeed.

Overall, though, people just simply seem to adore Sophia. Why? Maybe it's that Sophia's so little and Dorothy is so big, yet Sophia puts her down. Maybe it's Sophia's sheer irreverence. When Dorothy's not being kind, Sophia will tell her to shut up, to stop acting like a pinhead. How many mothers would like to say the same thing to *their* grown-up children but wouldn't dare? Sophia is kind of like the bully who comes along and beats up the bully who's beating up on you.

I think a big part of Sophia's appeal is that our writers, who are absolutely brilliant, have made her so real and accessible. I don't think anybody would be afraid to walk over to Sophia and just start chatting. People see the character and think, I could talk to that lady. She plays it as it lays. How many people would walk up to Joan Collins on the street and say something like "Alexis? I was wondering, wherever did you pick up your earrings?"

I'm not certain why so many people seem to love Sophia. But it's wonderful.

There is one thing that Sophia and I have in common. We're both very short.

The other thing I share with her is this: underneath it all we care, about the people we love and their happiness, about the events going on in the world. Even when Sophia's barbs lean toward gratuitous, I always try to let the audience know that; yes, she may be saying this, but she doesn't really mean it. I always work with the love of the character.

I like Sophia. She's got a lot of heart. She's fearless. She looks damn good in a miniskirt.

But is she a role model?

I hear the question a lot—frankly, it makes me kind of uneasy. On one hand it's flattering, to both me and the writers. But every time I hear the term *role model*, I have to stop and think, Wait, Sophia's not a real person. She's a character on a TV show. So was Mister Ed.

At the same time, though, I can see how senior citizens can look at her and feel good. I like the fact that she has opinions, she's feisty, she makes her wants and needs known. And if watching Sophia reminds people that they can still be vital, vociferous, and vigorous, then I'm all for it.

One man always writes me from prison. He signs off each letter the same way: though he's considerably younger than I, he'd love to meet me. First, though, he wants to see me in a bathing suit. Could I please send a photo?

4
Let's Do Lunch:
Surviving Hollywood

Somehow, it seems I've become this celebrity person. At first it was too unreal even to consider. Me? A celebrity? *Now?*

But as "The Golden Girls" got hotter and hotter, and I stumbled along for the ride, the notion came over me slowly: when people let you stand in the "10 Items or Less" line with 22 items, it's clear that something has changed.

Now that I've "made it" after all those years, people want to know if my old crowd treats me differently. I think this story says it all:

After six months of doing "The Golden Girls," I

made my first trip back to New York. My second day home I encountered a neighbor.

"Where have you been?" she asked. "I haven't seen you for weeks."

"Actually," I said, "it's been six months."

"So, where have you been?"

"I've been in Hollywood."

She paused. "Is that anyplace near Lauderdale?"

"No, I mean Hollywood, California."

"Really? I have a cousin who moved out there 20 years ago. She just loves it."

At which point she turned and left.

Celebrity is a whole different package when it comes at my age. After living your life one way for so many years, it's not so easy to get with the revised program.

I went out to dinner one night with my son Barry and his wife, Alison, and there was a lady at a nearby table whose hair was green. What unnerved me was that she kept staring at me. I mean *really* staring.

Finally I whispered to Barry, "Why does that lady keep staring at me? She's the one with green hair."

"What do you mean?" Barry said. "She's looking at you because you're Estelle Getty."

It had never occurred to me.

That's because I don't see myself as a celebrity. I still see myself as this lady from Queens.

I love living in Hollywood, though. I love the sunshine, the palm trees, the slower pace. All in all, it's a pretty nice joint.

It can also be quite entertaining. Especially if you're in "show biz."

We Golden Girls talk "show biz," although we do it in jest: "Let's do lunch . . . Why don't we do lunch? . . . I really think we should do lunch . . . Kiss-kiss, love youuuu." The funny thing is that people in Hollywood don't even talk that way. The only time you actually hear it is when someone's making fun of it. (If you *really* want to talk "Hollywood," you must master these three lines: "Is that my phone?" "Is this *brewed* decaf?" "Well, actually, we're in development.")

One thing about show business I noticed right away: success in this business means never having to do things for yourself. It's quite nice, especially for me; it's the first time in my life I've ever been catered to.

I don't know, maybe I just don't understand the scene. I *know* I don't understand one thing: this business of eating. Everyone in Hollywood is on a diet, yet they're all obsessed with the finest restaurants. They eat virtually nothing ("Oh, it's *very* nouvelle.") and spend a fortune for the privilege.

Not me. I pay. I eat. I get fat.

Besides, I can't keep track of all the fancy restaurants. So I take the easy way out: I go to the Sizzler.

I eat at the Sizzler all the time. They have great fresh salad, and I can eat it until my eyes bug out.

More Sizzlers!

Of course when my managers read this, they'll go

crazy: "What are you doing telling people you eat at the Sizzler?"

I know, I know, but I can't help it: I hate airs. I refuse to put on airs. Cultivating an image is to me like jogging: a waste of good energy. I meet everybody as myself. I may not be much, but I'm all I've got.

Besides, I happen to know that I'm not the only one in Hollywood who eats at the Sizzler. I recently met Lou Diamond Phillips, the fine young actor from *La Bamba* and *Stand and Deliver*.

He said, "You know, I almost came up and met you once."

I said, "Why didn't you?"

He said, "Well, I was too embarrassed. It was at the Sizzler."

Lou, baby, next time say hello. We'll do lunch.

Now that I've told you how swell and unaffected I am, in the spirit of honesty and balance and since you'll probably find out anyway, I have a confession.

I try hard not to get too big for my britches. Once in a while, though . . .

I was once in Florida on business with one of my managers, Alan. It was almost 4:00 P.M., and we hadn't had time for lunch, so we went to a local restaurant called the Rascal House. It's a popular place, but we figured since it was 4:00 in the afternoon, restaurant limbo, the place would be empty. Wrong. When we arrived, there was a long line of people. The Early Bird special. Half price.

Anyway, a few people in the line recognized me and came over to chat. Several more joined them. Then a few more. At that point, Alan went inside and found the host.

"Estelle Getty's outside in line," he said, "and a lot of people are coming over. It's becoming a scene. Maybe you could get us a table."

The host didn't exactly swoon. "I don't care who she is, she's waiting in line," he said. "Danny Thomas waits in line, she can wait in line."

When I heard that, I roared. I laughed even harder after I told the story to Tony Thomas, my boss and Danny Thomas's son. Tony told his father, and Danny's reply was "Tell her *I never* waited in line there."

Frankly, I don't need much to keep me humble—I think I have a realistic view of my ability and talent. I'm not being modest; I'm being honest. I think I'm okay.

Even if I thought I was the best actress in the world, people have a way of bringing you right back to earth. I was with my husband for dinner one night, and we were sitting at a table with three other couples we didn't know. My husband introduced us (using his name), and one of the ladies looked up.

"Oh my God," she said, "you look exactly like the lady on 'The Golden Girls.' "

A second lady said, "What's that?"

The first lady described the show, and the second lady said, yes, she had seen the show, and I did look just like the lady on "The Golden Girls." She said I even sounded like her. I was about to confess, when the woman had a revelation.

"I know who you are," she shrieked. "You're Barbara Bel Geddes!"

If you *really* want to understand how things work in Hollywood, I have to tell you about my little orange car.

When I moved to Hollywood, I quickly realized it was impossible to survive without a car. This was before "The Golden Girls," my poor period, so it made good sense when someone suggested a Toyota. I went to the lot and picked out a car, but the dealer said Toyotas were hot; it would be almost six weeks for delivery, four if I didn't care about the color.

I couldn't wait that long and started to leave, but on my way out I spotted this cute little used orange Toyota Tercel. It had only a few thousand miles; we haggled over the price, and I bought it.

I loved that little car. Like me, it was small, I could park it anywhere, and it was simple to spot—in a town of exotic cars, I could always pick out the little orange car and know it was mine. I was very happy.

Then I got "The Golden Girls," and just like that, I got my own parking spot on the studio lot! The first

time I drove up and saw the sign on my space—
"Reserved for Estelle Getty"—I got this shiver of
satisfaction: *Well, kid, this is it. You've finally made
it.*

Then I took a closer look at the sign. It was one of
those stick-on things. The kind you can peel right
off.

"The Golden Girls" was a hit, though, and I got to
keep my space. Every Friday people jammed into the
parking lot to see us tape the show, and when they
arrived, this is what they saw: Rue's Mercedes Benz,
Bea's BMW, one of two vintage Cadillacs belonging
to Betty . . . and this little orange Tercel.

People started coming up to me in the hall: "Estelle, I'm sorry to tell you this, but someone took
your parking space. There's a Toyota in your spot."

"No," I'd say. "No one took my spot. That's my
car."

They would grin, certain that I was joking. When
they realized I wasn't, they were aghast.

A year passed, the show became a megahit, and
still I was driving the Tercel. My managers and
agents were getting upset. I understood how they
felt, but I also decided they were being silly. I knew
I made enough money to afford a better car, and
they knew it, so why did I have to show everyone
else?

"Don't worry," I told them. "When you're poor
and you do strange things, people think you're
crazy. When you make good money and do strange

things, people just think you're eccentric. Let them think I'm eccentric."

So everyone thought I was eccentric. I'm not, but I didn't care. By then the damn car was a point of honor.

Then, at the end of the year, I got a call from my business manager, Matt Lichtenberg.

"Are you still driving that Toyota?" he said.

"Yes, I am," I sighed. I was about to repeat my standard defense of my little car when he surprised me.

"Well, it's now depreciated fully," he said. "There's nothing I can deduct anymore. You have to buy a new car."

Now we weren't talking image; we were talking a language I could understand. Now we were talking money.

So what kind of car should I get? I knew it wouldn't be a Mercedes or a Cadillac or a BMW. While I have great regard for those cars, I can't see over the wheel. All my life I've had to sit on phone books or big fat pillows while driving. One time Arthur fixed up a car for me by putting blocks beneath the seat to raise it. It worked great until other people had to park it and they kept hitting their heads on the roof.

So I looked and I looked, and finally I found this Acura Legend. I bought it for one reason: the seat went up and down and forward in about 19 positions. I wouldn't have to use books or pillows.

I like my new car, but it also boggles my mind. It's all electric with a million buttons I've had to learn how to use. So now I tool around L.A. in this spaceship. The little orange Toyota? Out of sheer orneriness, I refuse to get rid of it.

The fuss about my little car showed me something: in Hollywood, if people think you're a "star," they expect you to spend like one.

I was once planning a dinner party for 40 people, and everyone told me I had to get a caterer. Okay, I figured, for this I'll "go Hollywood." I'll get a caterer.

I called the caterer, and she described what sounded like a nice dinner party, with hors d'oeuvres and a hot dinner and dessert and wine and beer. Then she told me what it would cost. I thought I'd heard wrong. When she repeated it, I thought she'd lost her mind.

"You can never do a party for less than that," she said.

"You bet your pants I can. And I intend to," I said.

"Well, what do you think you're going to do?"

"Whatever it is I'm going to do, I'm not going to spend thousands of dollars on dinner for 40 people. It's ridiculous."

"Well," she said, "if you want to have anything decent . . ."

"I guess I'll just have to have something indecent."

It was pure lunacy, and I refused to get sucked in. I wound up making half the dinner myself and buying the rest from a very good restaurant. The caterer was wrong: it was a great party.

I don't think money can buy you happiness. But I do think it makes a respectable down payment.

People ask me, "Now that you've got some money, does money have less meaning?"

No. I lived through the Depression, and it shaped who I am. I've never forgotten the Depression. I'm still waiting for the next one, when they'll take all my money away.

Oh, I'll spend money, but it took me many years of therapy to feel that it was okay to buy something just because I *wanted* it, not because I *needed* it. One thing in my life has never changed: if it's a bargain, I want it.

That's why I spend a lot of time at the La Brea Circus in Los Angeles. It's kind of hard to describe . . . let's just say it's beyond flea market. Most of the time the stuff doesn't work, but when it does you can really make out. Need an oven mitt from Guam? Three hundred off-brand pickles for a dollar? If you can dream it, La Brea Circus has got it.

It does have its limitations. You go into a normal store to buy some cheese, the expiration date isn't for four months. You go to La Brea Circus, find the same cheese for a tenth of the price—and it expires later that day. If you're a fast eater like me, it's still a hell of a bargain.

My problem is I have no restraint when it comes to bargains. I'll see some Nova Scotia lox, normally very expensive, and buy several pounds. A bargain! Then I'll get home, realize I've got all this lox that expires tomorrow, and figure I'd better hurry and invite some friends for brunch. By the time I've bought all the eggs and the bagels and juice and milk and everything else, I've spent a hundred bucks. All because I found some cheap lox.

My friends kid me to death. Anytime I can't be found for a couple of hours, they're sure I've been to La Brea Circus. I don't mind. I love odd things, and it's got the oddest. The best thing I ever bought there was this really sexy, merry-widow corselette. It's red, it's got garters, I've never worn it, and I probably never will.

What a deal, though.

* * * * * *

I was once in Chicago, and a lady came running at me, full force, like she might tackle me. First I got nervous. Then I realized she meant no harm—she was a big fan of the show.

"I have to hug you! I have to hug you!" she shouted. Then she smothered me in a bear hug and lifted me off the ground.

That type of incident is not as rare as you might guess. Even when people don't know me, they feel like they do. Every Saturday night I come into their homes. People see me in my bedroom, in the bathroom, in the kitchen. When you see a person eating and washing and lounging in her nightgown, of course you feel she's someone you know.

As long as no one gets too rough, I like the attention I get. (I think all actors do, even the ones who seemingly shun it.) But it takes some getting used to, at least for a people watcher like me. Suddenly you're not the observer, but the observee.

Once I was trying on a dress in a fitting room, and I asked the saleswoman if she could bring me a smaller size. As I spoke, another shopper recognized my voice.

"Oh my God," she said, "you're Estelle Getty. You've got to wait right here. I've got to go and get my mother. She's right outside!"

Before I knew it, a crowd of women surged into my fitting room, wanting autographs. That was fine, except the saleswoman hadn't returned with the other dress. I was standing there, blushing, in my ripped pantyhose and bra.

Unlike some celebrities, I don't get this all the time. I'm not mobbed wherever I go, because I don't look like Sophia. Unless I speak, I often go unrecognized. Most times people will have a vague flash of recognition. They'll look at me, shrug, scratch their head, and I can practically see them thinking. *Where do I know her from? Is she from my neighborhood or what?*

Most people who approach are polite, even shy. They'll hop around and try to get their nerve up to say hello, which I always find sweet and amazing. It's rare that people are rude. Even when they appear to be, I think it's just that they're overly anxious.

Arthur and I were in a restaurant once when a lady hurried up to our table. I had a fork in my hand, almost in my mouth, and she grabbed my wrist.

"I know you're eating," she said, "but I'm such a big fan of yours, and I want you to sign these two cards for me."

Somehow, Arthur managed not to flog her with a Ry-Krisp. He looked at her calmly and said, "Would you please let go of my wife's wrist?"

She let go. She didn't even realize she was doing it.

Though I've never refused an autograph or a conversation, and I never will, I'd be lying if I told you I *always* like the attention. There are days— maybe I have a cold, or I just woke up and my hair is composed in some strange geometric shape—when all I want to do is complete my little errand and get back home. My civilian friends don't seem to understand this; my sister Roz is the worst. She'll walk into a bank and tell the guard, "That's my sister. She's Estelle Getty."

I'll tell her, "Roz, say one more word to anyone

on the street, and I'll punch your heart out."

It can be embarrassing, but it's also special. Our show is fortunate to have such terrific fans; people send us all kinds of offbeat items—someone once sent Betty a six-foot stuffed dog. We get all kinds of wonderful things: lucky dice and bookmarks and banners and flags and sweatshirts and flowers.

Mostly people send letters. I get letters from people of all ages, but for some reason more than half of my mail comes from kids. I don't know, maybe it's my size, maybe kids love to see someone little put down someone big like Bea Arthur.

I also get a lot of letters from older people, lots of widowed men, especially men who are Italian (since Sophia's Italian, people tend to think I am too).

"I'm a widower," one sweet man wrote, "and I'd like to meet a nifty lady like you."

He invited me to go with him to his small, obscure Italian town and hinted that marriage might not be out of the question. He said he realized I might be just a touch crazy, but he was well into his eighties and deaf enough not to notice.

One man always writes me from prison. He signs off each letter the same way: though he's considerably younger than I, he'd love to meet me. First, though, he wants to see me in a bathing suit. Could I please send him a photo?

Which proves he's not just a convict, he's also nuts.

The first few weeks of retirement are great. Then they have golf balls and fish coming out of their ears. You see these men who used to have so much status and responsibility, and now they're lost souls. Every two minutes they poke their heads into the kitchen and ask their poor wives, "Should I go and buy bananas?"

5
Men, Marriage, and Sex (Not Necessarily in That Order)

If love means never having to say you're sorry, marriage means having to say everything twice.

It's true. You live with your roommates or your parents and you say, "Did I get any mail?" And they say, "Yes" or "No." At least you get an immediate response.

It's very different when you're married. When you're married you say, "Did I get any mail, *did I get any mail?*" Or "Do you want lamb chops, *do you want lamb chops?*" Say things once, you don't have a chance; husbands, due to some undiscovered quirk of the universe, never hear you the first time.

How else do you know you're married? When the honeymoon ends, all the things he kept to himself during the courtship he now feels free to dump on you. Like, your stuff in the bathroom is where he wants to put *his* stuff. Like, he lied when he said he liked your single friends. Like, the sight of you in curlers causes nausea. Take it from a veteran, these are all reliable signs.

Marriage is knowing someone better than he knows himself. You wake your husband in the middle of the night, tell him he's snoring like the Missing Link, and he tells you you're crazy—goddamn it, he doesn't snore!—even as the neighbors shriek, "Earthquake!"

Arthur, my husband, is left-handed, and very early on I learned to put his coffee cup on his left-hand side. Now every time we eat in a restaurant he asks, "How come that waiter puts my coffee on the right-hand side?"

It all looks rosy when you're on your honeymoon. We drove to upstate New York and stayed in a beautiful hotel in the mountains. The only problem was, the room next door was packed with a raucous group of vacationing men who drank and caroused and never seemed to sleep. Finally they got so loud we complained to the management. The next day we saw them and they knew we were the ones who had turned them in. But to our surprise, they were quite friendly. A fun group of guys. That night, as we fell asleep, there was a sharp banging on our wall.

"Leave that boy alone," they screamed at me. "The guy's losing weight. He looks terrible. Let the poor guy get some rest."

Good advice, which we didn't heed or need.

Once the glow of the honeymoon dimmed, I'm not sure Arthur was prepared for what he was getting into by marrying me. You have to understand, he has two brothers whose marriages bear no resemblance whatsoever to the one that Arthur would have. Consider, for instance, "You Know Herb" and "Poor Ruth."

Herb is Arthur's older brother, a man who has never pulled a punch in his life, a man who, if he met the pope, would probably say, "What's with the big hat?" Ruth, his saintly wife, is always cast in the role of Herb's defender. So every time someone complains about Herb, poor Ruth says, "You know Herb. He just says things, he doesn't mean them. You know Herb."

Poor Ruth, You Know Herb.

Arthur is the only one of his brothers who married outside the "faith": his brothers married sweet, docile, attending women of the old school; Arthur got a feminist with a mouth. Oh, I did the cooking and the cleaning and all the rest of the chores that women of my generation were programmed to do, but I was never as accommodating as Ruth or Maurice's Mary Agnes. Had Arthur married such a woman, I'm sure his life would have been much easier.

Yet we've stayed together and raised two great sons. And in today's divorce-crazy environment, couples like us (who've been married since Lincoln was clean-shaven) often get asked the secret to a long marriage. After 40 years of wedlock I've discovered the answer: I wasn't home half the time.

To keep the peace with Arthur, I learned never to tell him I had fun if I went somewhere without him, unless it was someplace like the dry cleaner, in which case I could tell him I had the time of my life. But if it was a weekend with friends in the country and Arthur couldn't go, God forbid I should rave. I did that once, and for a week Arthur treated me like I was the IRS. After that, even if I'd been schussing in the Alps with Di and Fergie, I'd yawn and tell him it was "reasonable."

Believe me, Arthur has his own strategies for détente. He's the sole life form on this planet that thinks I'm great-looking. I used to point to women who were many times more attractive than I was, and he'd say they paled in comparison to me. I'd argue the point, but not too strongly.

He has also been supportive of my career. Though I always had a "regular" job as an executive secretary, I did it of my own volition—I felt it was only right that I pitch in. But if acting jobs ever got scarce and I became discouraged, Arthur would tell me to quit my job and concentrate only on my theatrical career. His support, emotional and financial, never wavered. Had it not been for Arthur, I probably never could have accomplished what I did.

For that I'm very grateful.

I see young people madly in love, drunk with visions of fairy-tale romance and happily-ever-afters. And I say, "Great, romance is lovely. But it doesn't mean a thing if you don't have friendship."

Nothing matters more in a marriage than friendship. Everything else—great sex, great looks, great sex—will eventually fade. But friendship endures. It is, I believe, the *only* relationship that endures, and the most perfect ingredient for a marriage, or any relationship, for that matter. If we treated our spouses, our sweethearts, our parents, our children, as we treat our best friends, with the same forgiveness and tolerance and forbearance, we would all be better for it. You would never shout at a friend, "My God, your behind . . . it's the size of Pittsburgh!"

How do you find that best friend to grow old and prematurely gray with? I say look for common ground. I've never accepted the theory that opposites attract, at least not for the duration. In fact, I think the thing that excites you most about an opposite is precisely what will eventually repel you. It's like the man who marries the very sexy woman—you know, tight pants, push-up bras, short skirts, high heels, lots of bosom. At first he's smitten. In time he's screaming, "Once in your life, can't you wear a turtleneck?"

The closer people are in age, race, religion, and background, the better their chances for a marriage that will pass the test of time. I am absolutely, positively sure about this . . . I think.

People frequently ask me how Arthur feels about the fact that I've had to relocate to Los Angeles from New York due to my career. And I tell them: the same way I would feel if he had to leave home for his career. It's not that I like having a phone bill that rivals the national debt. But I'm an actress. I go where the work is.

Some people have a hard time with this. They assume that a wife must have her husband's permission to leave home because of her work—after all, that's the way it's been since time immemorial.

Why the double standard? Male entertainers go on the road, no one says boo. Men in many professions go away for months at a time, and no one questions that. But if it's the woman who leaves, she's not only questioned, she's judged. Even some of my close friends, relatively liberated women, would not pursue their careers beyond the parameters of New York, for fear their husbands would not allow it.

Perhaps they were right. I just know for *me* it would be wrong. Arthur has never asked me to forgo acting jobs to stay at home, and I've never asked him to alter his lifestyle to accommodate mine.

He is also at ease with my so-called fame, which I know isn't always typical. Most men, it seems to me, identify themselves by their profession much more than women do (at least women of my generation). Ask men to describe themselves and they say, I'm a lawyer, I'm a plumber, I'm a jockey. Ask women and they'll probably say, I'm a mother, I'm a wife, I do volunteer work for the Red Cross. If a wife's profession has a higher profile than her husband's, it can be a problem.

Arthur has insecurities, but not in this area. He's proud of me, not threatened, even when people call him Mr. Getty, which is not his last name. He could move out to Los Angeles, but he's not in show business and he isn't keen on the glitz, the parties, the kiss-kiss love-you-babys. It's not him. I've never tried to make it him.

Besides, Magic Johnson runs less than I do. I work the equivalent of a nine-to-five day on the show and usually attend a benefit or some sort of function for business or fun several times a week. I keep late hours and constantly have to study lines. It's not a great lifestyle for a man who likes company.

So now Arthur lives down in Florida near his brothers, our son Carl, my sister Roz, lots of cousins and friends, and his transplanted business. It isn't the best way to have a marriage, but it isn't the worst. We vacation together and we see each other

more than people would expect. We've been together for 40 years. We're okay.

Am I giving you the impression I never fight with
my husband? If so, I'm giving you the wrong impression.

One thing I will say in our defense: we never fight
about the little things. It has to be something mean-
ingful, with serious ramifications. Like where to go
out to eat.

We have this argument, oh, about every time we
go out to eat. We'll wait until the last possible
minute, until we're famished and irritable, and then
it goes something like this:

"You tell me," Arthur will say. "Anywhere you
want to go."

"Really? How nice. Let's go to Chico's."

"I can't go there; the food's too spicy."

"Then why'd you ask me?"

"I wanted to please you."

"Okay, let's eat Italian."

"I'll go, but I won't feel well."

"Fine, let's eat Chinese."

"Chinese, huh? Yeah, that's . . . great."

Arthur's "great" will hang in the air like a lead
balloon, and we'll be back to square one. We'll do
this for 10, 15 minutes, then eat at the Springfield
Diner, the same place we do every time we go out.

Ring any bells?

We also fight over movies. Oh, we agree to see the

same one, but that's the last thing we agree on. From that point on it's the Great Debate. Tell me: why is it that I can acknowledge Arthur's views, but Arthur, like many men, feels I *must* come around to his way of thinking? "No," I keep saying, "I'm sticking to my opinion." And still he'll nag me until my teeth ache. The only way to stop him is to say, "Enough, I don't want to discuss this, I'm going to bed!" Or else I put in my curlers. That stops him every time.

One thing we *always* fight about is Arthur's clothes. I'm always trying to improve his wardrobe. He always retorts, "Don't try to dress me like those women down in Miami dress *their* husbands. Don't even try."

I know what he means. In Miami, all the men look exactly alike. They all have short white hair, brown rim glasses, and are 10 to 25 pounds overweight. On Monday they all have on little blue shorts and little blue shirts and little blue socks—and white walking shoes. On Tuesday it's little yellow shorts and little yellow shirts and little yellow socks—and white walking shoes. Wednesdays it's pink, then green, and so on, until the cycle starts over.

These are retired men and women whose children have grown and moved away, and for years the wives have had no one left to dress, so now they dress their husbands, which is kind of nice. The husbands don't work, so now they can wear pink and yellow and blue, and they look darling.

There *is* a problem with this. Sometimes I see these women looking around frantically in this sea of pastel, each trying to identify her very own "flamingo."

Arthur the renegade says he will *never* dress like that. And he won't: he'll always be wearing his cutoffs with his belly folded over his belt.

* * * * * *

The check is in the mail.

I'll respect you in the morning.

Men are tougher than women.

Uh-huh. Sure.

Men tougher than women? That's a good one. Men are stronger, they do war things better and fix pipes better and know more about calculating mortgage rates while watching All-Star wrestling. But they sure as hell are not tougher.

There's a funny story about a man who asks his wife whether childbirth was hard.

She says, "Honey, pull out your lip."

He pulls out his lip.

"Now pull it out as far as it can go."

He pulls it out as far as it can go.

"Okay," he says, "now what?"

She smiles.

"You want to know what childbirth feels like? Pull your lip over your head. *That's* what childbirth feels like."

Someone once said if a man had the first child in

every family, every family would have only one child. I believe that's true. In all fairness, I also believe if women could *remember* what it was like to have that first child. . . .

No, men are not tougher than women. Just different. Very, very different.

I have a real thing about how men and women perceive things. I really think that the average man, no matter how intelligent, is not terribly perceptive and will never notice all the things that most women do. Men just don't pick up nuances that women spot immediately. You go to a party with your husband and it's clear as a bell: the host and hostess aren't speaking . . . the man near the piano is cheating on his wife (why else the toupee and the midwinter tan?) . . . one woman has gained 10 pounds . . . another has lost 25 . . . the man talking to your husband has the worst set of caps ever made and can't stop smiling. After the party you're in the car and you tell your husband everything you've seen. And he says, "Huh? . . ."

That's because men see only the big picture. Unlike women, men never see the minutiae. A woman will walk into a room, take one glance at a plant, and know if it's fake or real. A man will say, "I don't know—it looks pretty nice to me."

I also find it amusing that Arthur can look in a mirror and see only that part of himself he wants to see. He'll look at his hair—it's white and attractive, he's a nice-looking man—and he'll walk away from the mirror feeling perfectly content, never noticing the collar of his jacket, which happens to be turned under.

I look in the mirror and call the vice squad. I see every mark, every blemish, every wrinkle. When you're with me, if there's one thing you needn't be shy about, it's my looks. Sometimes a friend will delicately try to point out some new physical short-coming, and I'll say, "It's okay, kid. I saw it before you did."

Another thing: men always think their mothers were right. About what it doesn't matter—it could be Mozart or mayonnaise. The point is, their mothers were *right*—and don't you dare forget it. A man can tell a brutally funny story about his mother's cooking, but when his wife repeats the story verbatim, he books a spot on "Divorce Court."

Now that I'm rolling, why do men refuse to throw things out? Unless of course those things belong to you, because then they must be frivolous bordering on trash. Men will cling to old shoes they never wear, old books they will never get around to reading, old pants that now don't fit over their ankles let alone their waists. I know men who have statements from banks that have long been replaced by Dairy Queens.

Men are just as stubborn when it comes to shopping. Nine times out of ten they just refuse to go, and the one time they do, you wish they hadn't—

they're miserable, and they make you miserable. I always stare in wonder at that rare, dear sweet soul who holds his wife's coat and purse while she tries on clothes. This is usually the same man who can cut his wife's hair and dry a dish. A man who can distinguish paprika from Drano. I always wonder, Where did she find this treasure, and how did she train him to do that? Donahue, I imagine, is such a man.

Most men are nothing like Donahue. There are entire worlds that most men know nothing about. For openers, grocery shopping. Men get very confused when they have to shop by themselves. They have no clue about proportion. If you send a man to buy cream cheese for a cake, plus some salt, he'll come back with an ounce-and-a-half of cream cheese and five pounds of salt. There's only one thing you can bet on: cookies. Lots of cookies and a gallon of ice cream in a flavor nobody but he likes.

Driving with men . . . that's no day at the tanning booth. Men will not ask for directions. They will drive for seven days, grow a beard, and wear out their tires (not to mention their wives) before they'll break down and ask for directions. I guess asking directions isn't macho, but being lost somehow is. Most men would rather drive into the ocean than ask directions to the beach.

I suppose I'm partially to blame: if I could read a road map, the men I drive with wouldn't have to ask for directions. But I can't; my mind simply won't access road map information. My husband knows this and still depends on me to read them, even though I cry and carry on and beat him over the head with the goddamn maps.

Arthur, however, does get us where we want to go . . . eventually. Once we were on our way from New York to North Carolina, and I asked him if we were on the right road.

"Don't worry," he said. "We're going in the right general direction." To Arthur, south is south.

This is fine if you've always had a yen to see Georgia. If you're late for a party in Great Neck, it's kind of a drag.

* * * * * *

"I'd like to have sex," says a man to his wife on a Wednesday.

"I can't," says his wife. "I have this terrible head-ache."

"I'd like to have sex," says the man on Thursday.

"I'm sorry," she says. "I just had my hair done."

"I'd like to have sex," says the man on Friday.

"I'm exhausted," says his wife. "I've been cleaning the house and cooking all day."

Now it's Saturday, time to unwind, the pressures of the week dissolved, and the man approaches his wife with newfound hope.

"I'd like to have sex," says the husband.

"What are you?" says the wife. "Some kind of sex maniac?"

It's an old joke, and it raises an old question: do men really want sex more than women?

As far as I'm concerned, it's a question that can't be answered. I agree that in every male/female relationship, someone wants sex more than his or her partner. But "someone" does not necessarily mean the man. Sexy ladies feel the same way about sex as sexy men do. Repressed men feel the same way about sex as repressed ladies do. It's a question of hormones, not gender.

Where men and women differ is not in how much sex they want, but in how gracefully they accept *criticism* of how much sex they want. Women, in this particular area, are much less sensitive than men. If a man's partner complains she's not sexually fulfilled, for him it's a traumatic, emasculating, monumental crisis, equivalent to rain washing out the entire World Series.

I think men worry way too much about how good they are at sex. It isn't their fault. In the old days, men and women decided for themselves if their sex lives were healthy. Not today. Now the media decide. We're relentlessly bombarded with all this sexual advice. This is good sex, this is bad sex, and if God forbid you've been doing your sex the same way, even if every repetitious second has been kind of terrific, we feel sorry for you. People who've been perfectly satisfied with their sex lives for years are now being told they only *think* they're satisfied.

This to me is ridiculous. People have their own sexual needs. My sexual "problem" may be your Fourth of July. Who's to arbitrate?

It's not that the people giving the advice aren't necessarily qualified. Dr. Ruth, for instance, is a very competent analyst and a woman I like a lot. But I wonder if anyone takes her seriously. Treating sexual problems on the phone, over the air, in front of a room full of people, is comical by nature. And perhaps misleading. How can anyone treat intricate sexual problems that may have taken years to manifest with tidy, over-the-phone solutions?

Besides, when someone comes to you with a sexual problem, is he or she really coming to you with just a sexual problem? My own experience with people is that nothing is ever what it sounds like. Women say their husbands don't engage in foreplay, or men complain of frigid wives. Now, does the complaining wife admit she comes to bed in curlers and a parka? Does the husband mention he's just awakened a young mother who's been up since 4 A.M attending to their feverish child? Of course not.

I don't get it. How can anyone pass judgment on something so personal and involved? Advice is easy. It's the problems that are hard.

Finding someone you like is not easy. It takes

intuition and savvy. The best bet, I think, is to follow your instincts. If you're a healthy person, you'll look for another healthy person.

But I would also look for the little things. Does he treat the waiter like dog food and leave his tips in change? Does he curse and perspire when the valet is eight seconds late with the car? Does he blame "bad luck" for everything that's wrong with his life?

If the answers are yes, I say dump him.

Don't go out with anyone who sees everything in life in terms of money. If he goes to a buffet and takes five cuts of prime rib even if he's a vegetarian, dump him.

Don't date someone who has no civility, no finesse, no regard for other people's opinions. If you go to a movie and afterward you say you thought it was kind of cute and he says, "You cow, all you know about film you could stick in a pigeon's eye and it wouldn't go blind!"—dump him. Quickly.

Beware of someone who doesn't listen. Who must have immediate gratification. Who doesn't like your family, who lies, who ever handled you with any but loving intentions. Dump him.

Habitual lateness is another bad sign. This is a biggie. I think lateness is an indication of not caring. If you've been dating for a year and you've never seen the opening act of a play, give him a karate chop. Then dump him.

I went to see a friend of mine, a lovely, wonderful woman in her late fifties, who was dating a man I had never met, also in his fifties. He was very attractive.

I said to him, "I must tell you I have enormous regard for you. Most men as attractive as you would be going with someone half your age."

He said, "I did that. How many years can you hold in your stomach?"

He went on to tell me about his dates with younger women after his divorce and how they never worked out. How after dinner and a movie, he was ready to go to sleep and his dates would want to go *dancing*.

"Now I date women my own age," he said. "We've got the same problems."

I found this interesting, because it's rare that you hear anything like it. Especially in Hollywood, where you see many older men dating and marrying younger ladies who are terribly attentive to them. I often wonder, do these men with their grizzly gray hair and flabby chests and Q-tip legs believe that these gorgeous, firm-thighed, full-bosomed young women are fatally attracted to them? Do they honestly think the relationship is fueled by sex and not by the two strongest aphrodisiacs in the world, money and power?

My guess is yes and yes.

Not that I find anything wrong with older men dating younger women. I don't. I just think it's good to be realistic about it, and this is another area where I find women to be much more honest with themselves than men. Women my age love to look at young men with broad chests and full heads of hair; we may be old, but we're not dead. But older women don't kid themselves. An older woman knows a younger man will see her body and his blood pressure won't exactly race. She knows her body won't measure up to the body of a young girl. She knows there may be many reasons that a younger man might want to date her, and sex may or may not be one of them.

But why does an older man think a younger woman wants to date *him*?

Obviously. He's a love machine. Or so he thinks. Dumb.

Southern mothers are subtle. They smile sweetly while they nag, and they nag you in that soft, melodious southern accent. It's quiet, it's lovely— and they will softly and sweetly nag you to death. They'll nag you until you have migraines, until you're kneeling on the floor with busted knee-caps, pleading, "Stop! I'll do it! I'll be a doctor *and* an attorney!"

6
Secrets of a
Professional Mother

Don't ever challenge me to a nagging contest:
I'll wind up with your house.

After all, I'm a mother.

I've been a mother for a lot of years—I take it
seriously. Acting is my job, it's what I do, but it's not
what I *am*. My children are the most important part
of my life. My children come before anything.

I have not lived the most traditional, typical life,
but when it came to raising my children, I was old-
fashioned. Even when they were small and my acting career was crucial to me, it was even more
crucial that my children never be deprived of hav-

ing a mother. So I had four distinct jobs: mother, wife, secretary, actress. I'd cook and clean and iron and vacuum, and I'd run back and forth to my secretarial job and keep in touch with my agent, Monty Silver. At night, after my kids were put to bed, I would run out to be an actress.

I worked hard at being a mother because I wanted to and it was what I knew—my mother was one of the hardest-working women I've ever known. That doesn't mean, though, that motherhood came naturally simply because I was a mother. To me, "motherhood" is a myth. I've never believed that women become maternal simply through the act of giving birth. Women learn to be mothers. They grow into the job.

Conversely, I know childless women who are extremely maternal. Betty White is one of the most nurturing, mothering women I know, whether she's caring for people or animals. Betty's never had her own children, but she's very much a mom.

Just as you never know what kind of mother someone will be, nobody can foretell what kind of kids one will have. Let's face it: having children is a crapshoot.

There are two areas in life for which there are no dependable criteria: the first is succeeding in show business; the second is how to raise the kind of children you want. In both instances you can take every precaution, give love, direction, and purpose, set the example, and you still wind up with two strangers who will give up partnerships in Dad's business to become professional surfers.

It's unavoidable: there are so many other forces, societal forces, that are stronger than parents. If there's anything in this world you can't predict, it's the future of a child.

That's why I hate to see parents torment and second-guess themselves when their kids don't turn out the way they dreamed. I know it's easier said than done, but I think parents should give themselves a break. Take the credit when they turn out perfect and blame your in-laws' genes when they don't.

*   *   *   *   *   *

I'm a mother.

I'm Jewish.

Therefore, I'm a Jewish mother.

But you don't have to be Jewish to be a Jewish mother. There's another type of mother who can out-Jewish-mother the Jewish mother.

Southern mothers.

There is a distinction. Jewish-Jewish mothers are blunt. They're dramatic. They're deeply committed to volume.

Southern mothers are subtle. They smile sweetly while they nag, and they nag you in that soft, melodious southern accent. It's quiet, it's lovely—and they will softly and sweetly nag you to death. They'll nag you until you have migraines, until you're kneeling on the floor with busted kneecaps, pleading, "Stop! I'll do it! I'll be a doctor *and* an attorney!"

I know of what I speak—I've witnessed the carnage. I once worked in a play with a nice young man named Lawrence who was from the South. Lawrence was feeling good at the time: his ulcer had healed, and he hadn't smoked a cigarette in 18 months.

Then his mother came for a visit.

"Lawrence," she'd say softly and sweetly, "you have your back to Miss Getty. That's rude. Now honey, why'd you wear that shirt? You know I didn't get to iron it. And I wish you hadn't worn green in the first place, dear. You know you look so much better in blue."

For five straight days this continued. By the time his mother left, Lawrence was back to smoking two packs a day, and his face had broken out.

Let's face it: southern, northern, black, white, Jewish, Protestant—nagging is a mother's right. Suffering you do to keep away the evil spirits. Nagging is a directive from God.

If you're a mother, you must take pride in your nagging. Give it 110 percent. In other words, if you're going to nag, nag with gusto.

I had my own favorite nag: *"I can't take much more of this!"* I usually said this on early Saturday morning, when I was trying to steal some sleep and my kids were shrieking and watching cartoons.

When that didn't work—and it didn't—I would move to the threats: "Mommy's coming." This meant that Mommy was not only coming, but was coming to hit them. I could yell this 30 or 40 times, with no effect whatsoever.

What can I say? My kids were very strong. Even *guilt* rarely worked.

Not that I ever stopped trying. Guilt is a mother's bread and butter.

I liked to mix it up, keep my kids off balance. Sometimes I'd go with the direct, bludgeon-to-the-head approach: intense sighing. Or else I told them *not* to be guilty. Whatever they decided to do, "It's fine with me."

I strongly endorse this method. Defy them to do things, and they'll fight you. Give them permission, and they'll suffer, because they'll know you don't mean it.

No child, though, will ever suffer like you will. Suffering is a mother's job. What you suffer about depends largely on which kid we're talking about. If you've got a shy kid, you suffer knowing he's being beaten up. An aggressive kid, you suffer knowing that he's going to beat up someone else's kid. A hotshot pitcher should study more. A bookworm needs more fresh air.

If you've mastered all these techniques, and still what your kid does best is give you migraines, you have only one recourse.

Blame it on your husband.

It's the only way. God knows, mothers do everything right. If anything goes wrong with your kids, it's your husband's fault, or his family's. No one on *your* side has ever done these things.

I had it relatively easy when my kids were young. They were friendly and honest children, and extremely intelligent—by age four they were dominating me at Candyland, Checkers, and all card games. Give or take a Saturday morning, they were easy children to raise.

Today my older son, Carl, is a writer, a computer programmer, as well as an inventor. Carl is probably the most brilliant, eclectic person I know. He's gentle, laughs easily, has a photographic memory, and a curiosity that's boundless.

My younger son, Barry, is a hippie in yuppie's clothing, an administrative engineer for a general contractor in New York. Very, very intelligent, also a writer, and like his mother, Barry worries a lot. He's also a great caretaker—Barry takes care of everyone and everything. He's the family problem solver and we depend on him.

My sons were good children. Now they're even better adults.

In the sixties they gave me hell on earth.

Both were only 16 when they each left for college, but it didn't take them long to embrace the Age of Revolution. Arrests, expulsions from school, hair, hair, and more hair—my two adventurous sons tried it all. Isn't it amazing how our lives change? I used to worry about getting them to Little League on time.

I remember one Friday I called Carl at Columbia University, and his roommate told me he was at the library. *Good*, I thought. *He's really applying himself.* When I called that night, Carl was still at the library. I called Saturday morning—still there. Finally I tried late that night: "Sorry, Mrs. G, Carl is still at the library." Studying on a Saturday night. I couldn't get over how industrious Carl was.

The next morning, I happened to glance at the Sunday *New York Times*, and there on page one . . . was Carl. At the library. Sitting outside on the windowsill. He and his friends had taken it over.

"Oh," I said, "that library."

It was a tense, crazy day. No one could get through to the library, including the mayor—the students had control of the switchboard and were taking no incoming calls. Then, somehow, a call got through. One of the students picked it up.

"Hey, Carl," he shouted. "It's your mother."

Carl said he was never so embarrassed in his life. I don't remember how I did it—I was so furious it's a blur—but somehow I got through when no one else could. Right there, in the middle of the Columbia revolution, I lambasted my son.

I wasn't angry that he was protesting. I was angry because he'd broken the law. I had always been political myself, dating all the way back to the thirties. More recently, I had marched against the same war Carl was protesting, although I did it by candlelight in Washington and New York. So a part of me found what my kids were doing to be courageous and important. The "mother" part, concerned for their futures, wanted to grab them by their ears and send them to their room.

I laugh when people ask whether my sons like their mother being on television.

"No," I say, "they were hoping I'd be a bag lady."

To be honest, though, it isn't always easy having a mom who's an actress.

Barry was about seven years old the first time he saw me act. I was in a play in which I had to take off my skirt. I'm sure the poor kid was extremely surprised to see his mother in public without a skirt on. For a while when people in the neighborhood asked him if I was his mother, he'd say, "No. She's not really my mom. I just know her."

Eventually, as my sons got older, they began to understand my job. They started to like the fact that their mother was an actress. It made their mom a little different.

Then "The Golden Girls" happened, and seemingly overnight, their mother was a "celebrity." You'd think it might be strange, yet my kids don't seem to have a single problem with it. They're very proud of me. Now they accost strangers on the street to announce that I'm their mother.

Lack of food makes Jewish people, at least this Jewish person, very insecure. Even if I'm not hungry, I must have access to food. If I have to make a trip of more than 15 blocks, I take along a piece of fruit. If I don't, I know in my heart I'll die of scurvy.

7

"So Eat Something":
The Art of Being Jewish

I was talking to a friend of mine who's Jewish. He said he was tired of dating; he wanted to meet a nice Jewish girl, get married, and start having babies.

"What about this woman you just started dating?" I asked him.

"She's not into that kind of thing," he said.

"No? Is she Jewish?"

"I really don't know."

"Take her to the beach," I told him. "If you can see the light between her thighs, she isn't Jewish."

My daughter-in-law, Alison, whose background is

very WASP, says one of the great things about being Jewish is that you get to talk loud. You can have huge fights and tell the people you love what you really think, and the moment the explosion ends, you can go on speaking to one another. (This is also characteristic of Italian families, which is another reason I love Sophia.)

I thought that was very funny, also very true.

You really want to know what you need to be Jewish?

Undying devotion . . . to food.

Maybe it's the result of a history of deprivation. Maybe it's from hearing "Eat—children are starving in Europe" 18 million times when we were children. Maybe we just like to nosh.

Whatever the cause, Jews and food are a very hot item. Lack of food makes Jewish people, at least this Jewish person, very insecure. To this day, even if I'm not hungry, I must have access to food. If I have to make a trip of more than 15 blocks, I take along a piece of fruit. If I don't, I know in my heart I'll die of scurvy.

Back in New York with our crowd, food was a full-time obsession. At breakfast we'd have animated debates over where to have lunch. At lunch we'd critique that morning's breakfast. We could even be driving to a funeral: "Are you going back to the house? You think they'll have food?"

Food heals all wounds. Jewish families will have a

dramatic, painful, and serious crisis, with heated debates and profound decisions made that affect lives. The minute the dust settles, someone is sure to say, "So, what do you wanna eat?"

Nothing, however, heals like chicken soup. I make very good chicken soup—no fat, very tasty—and at any given time you will find a jar in my freezer. When I make chicken soup, I make so much you can bathe in it.

No one can resist it, not even my sister Roz. I say "even" because Roz is the eighth wonder of the world: she's Jewish, but she actually stops eating when she's full. It's astonishing but true. When Roz visits me in California, I'll give her some applesauce with her dinner. After dinner I'll disappear into the kitchen. I'll return a few moments later, wearing this sly grin.

"Cake time."

Roz will be frowning. "Why didn't you tell me there was dessert? I just had applesauce."

I'll say, "It's okay, you can have cake too."

Roz will shake her head no. "I don't eat two steaks or two soups. Why should I have two desserts?"

I shouldn't be surprised. Roz doesn't even have to wear a panty girdle.

"I eat until I'm comfortable," Roz explains. "If I start to get uncomfortable, I stop eating."

Weird concept or what?

You Know You're Jewish When . . .

- You start wearing glasses when you're seven.
- You ask, "You want a drink?" (meaning milk, hot chocolate, coffee, tea, or soda), and you're shocked when someone asks for a Scotch.
- Most of your furniture is covered with plastic.
- You cook something different for each person in the house, and you eat what's left over.
- You clean the gas jets on the stove with a toothpick because the war against dirt is serious business.
- There are more books than toilet paper in the bathroom.
- Your kids eat only tuna fish and peanut butter in your house, but they'll eat anything and everything at their friends' houses. Then the parents tell you what great eaters your kids are.
- Your thumb is so ungreen that you kill artificial plants.
- Your corduroy pants are threadbare at the thighs and the calves.
- There's a piano in the house, and nobody plays.
- You put sour cream on everything.
- You've heard of Velveeta but never tasted it.
- The first time you date a blonde you don't ask her last name because you don't really want to know. That way you don't have to lie to your mother when she asks.
- You're 40, and your parents still don't know you hate carrots.

- You want a Mercedes-Benz, but you wish you were principled enough not to buy one.
- You can borrow your parents' car without promising to wash it first.
- Your father says, "Don't worry about getting a TV and carpeting when you get married. Your mother and I will see to that." And they do.
- Even when you're 45, every time you enter a car your parents say, "Be careful how you drive."
- No matter how thin you are, your mother thinks you should diet, but on holidays she makes you eat until your eyes bulge. "Eat now," she says. "You'll diet later."
- The first time you leave home every beverage seems to lack *oomph*, because all you ever drank was seltzer.
- Even if it's August and you're in Palm Springs, your mother insists you take a sweater, because "it might get cool."
- You advise your kids to stay away from the arts, get a profession, work hard, buy a house in Great Neck, marry a Jewish girl, and have a boy, a girl, and a boy.
- You go to a family wedding, and no one's standing at the bar because they're all into the hors d'oeuvres.
- You go to a restaurant and return the first three courses for being overdone, underdone, and not like your mother's.

Doctors must view hypochondriacs like me with a mixture of lust and dread. Lust because we pay for their Porsches, dread because we never leave them time to drive them.

8
Confessions
of a Hypochondriac

"Estelle," someone once asked me, "if there was one thing about yourself you could change, what would it be?"

"My addiction to fear and anxiety," I said.

"Anything else?" he asked.

"What?" I said. "That isn't enough?"

Fear is my constant companion. I wake up scared, I go to sleep scared. And yet, as an overachiever, I force myself to get out and *do*, to fully experience my life. But first I look over my shoulder.

I am often paranoid. I hate it, yet I'm powerless to overcome it: I can find conspiracy in rye toast. I was even worse when I was younger, when my children first left home. If there was an airplane crash in Poland, I would call to make sure Barry and Carl weren't on it.

Even today, on the set of "The Golden Girls," my paranoia persists. Every time the producers huddle, I know they're discussing me.

I'm also a runaway pessimist. I figure that if things don't work out, I won't be quite as disappointed because I didn't expect they would in the first place. I know, I know: I should try to be more optimistic. Believe me, I considered it. But I knew it wouldn't work out.

My greatest trauma is over people who are late. To me, people are never simply late. They're crushed beneath the wheels of a freight train.

I can't help it; this is who I am. Some people play racquetball. I worry. Even when things are going well, I worry about what might go wrong. And on those rare occasions when I have *nothing* to worry about, I worry about that. Otherwise the fear of the unknown—the fear of precisely how and when that parking structure will collapse on my head—is much too great. I prefer my catastrophies on the table.

Say, did I mention my hypochondria?

My entire life, I have no recollection of *not* being a hypochondriac. Even as a child, for me there was no such thing as a simple pimple; it was the prelude to a battery of tests rivaled only by NASA.

There was never any question. Mine would be a life of worry.

The nice thing was I had so much company. My mother, father, brother, sister—all fine hypochondriacs. We were a family that hypochondriacted together.

Have you ever been with a bunch of hypochondriacs? If you can somehow forget your imminent death, it's very entertaining.

"So? What have you got?"

"What have I got? You know what I've got. I've got chronic bronchitis."

"Bronchitis? Hah! Bronchitis is nothing. I've had that twice. Shingles! Now that's a disease."

I think doctors must view hypochondriacs like me with a mixture of lust and dread. Lust because we pay for their Porsches, dread because we never leave them time to drive them. One day I couldn't resist.

"Do you treat me differently?" I asked my doctor. "I mean, because by now you know I'm a galloping hypochondriac?"

"No," he said. "I treat my hypochondrical patients the same way I do my regular ones."

"Really? How kind of you."

"Don't thank me," he said. "Hypochondriacs get sick and die like everyone else."

Was I offended? I was eternally grateful.

All it takes is one "Hmmmmm" from my doctor,

and I automatically rewrite my will. I recall the time a rather brusque doctor found some nodules on my thyroid.

"Is it dangerous?" I asked.

"It could be. We'll have to take a test."

"Could it be cancer?"

"It's possible."

Then, of course, he left the room. By the time he returned, I was squeezing the last corpuscle of blood from the arm of my good friend David, who had been sitting in the waiting room but was now at my side. I had called him in to tell him I had 24 hours to live.

When the doctor returned, he was somewhat surprised to find David in the examining room.

"This is my friend," I explained. "He's comforting me because I'm scared to death."

"Why are you scared to death?" the doctor said.

"Because you said I had cancer."

Which he hadn't, of course. But hypochondriacs have very selective hearing.

Despite those flashes of greatness, I still don't measure up to the purest of the species, what I call the exquisite hypochondriac. When a doctor tells me I will live to see another day, I believe. When a doctor tells an exquisite hypochondriac she's fine, it's simply cause for greater alarm. She *knows* this doctor got his medical degree from a correspondence school that broadcasts classes on channel 96 at midnight.

No, I am not an exquisite hypochondriac.
But I'm working on it.

People ask me: "Estelle, now that you're a Golden Girl, a Hollywood celebrity, how has your life changed?"

That's simple. Now I go to doctors who charge more.

To be exact, I go to *Hollywood* doctors. You can always tell a Hollywood doctor: he's more handsome, better dressed, more deeply tanned, and his jogging suit costs more than your condo. And like Hollywood accountants and Hollywood lawyers, Hollywood doctors love their Hollywood connections.

It isn't only the Hollywood doctors; *everybody* loves show business. Back in New York, in a small town on Long Island, there is a picture of me on my dentist's wall. There are no other celebrity pictures on Dr. Cooperman's wall, just the one of me. The inscription beneath it: "Dentist to the Stars."

I love that.

I also love the fact that doctors pay more attention to me now that I'm a Golden Girl. Believe me, once they know you're on TV, whoo boy, strike up the Band-Aids.

You may think I resent this double standard. Absolutely not. As a person who needs doctors like a fat man needs Dove Bars, I have learned to be tolerant.

Then again, I suppose my entire view of doctors is a bit off center. To me, doctors are gods—very hard to get to know, but boy, do they have clout.

I am not an expert on many things. But after years of ailments real and imagined, after years of sitting in waiting rooms reading eight-month-old *People* magazines, I am an expert on one thing: The Routine.

It doesn't matter who's the doctor, the lowliest schlepper or the very top heart man. The Routine goes like this:

The receptionist is very specific: you must be there at *exactly* 1:15. So you get there at 1:10 and proceed to wait until 1:45, *if* you're lucky. Then the nurse comes to get you and says, "Mrs. Getty, the doctor will see you now," which of course is not true. You sit all alone in the examining room, legs dangling from the table, wearing a paper Handi Wipe that barely covers your navel, and you wonder why they didn't leave you in the outer room—where at least you can sit and wonder what everyone *else* has—until the doctor pronounces himself ready.

So there you sit for three-quarters of an hour and the doctor finally makes an appearance, very businesslike and without a trace of apology for being late.

"Hello, how are you?" he asks.

"Very cold and very lonely," I answer.

Then, just as you're about to launch into the

multitude of things that ail you, he blurts those seven inevitable words: "Would you excuse me for a moment?"

He leaves to see another patient. Maybe three other patients. You sit. Sit some more. He comes back. He looks at this, looks at that, says "Um-hum, um-hum, um-hum—put on your clothes and come to my office. Where we can talk."

This is the death sentence—"come into my office." And you know you should have come with three people who can carry your degenerating body to the nursing home. But you get dressed and sit in his office. You sit some more. You sweat like a sumo wrestler. You memorize his diplomas.

After 15 minutes he reappears, and all of a sudden he's friendly. You're suspicious. He asks you all these questions about your family. Aha! He wants to see your family so he can tell them you're going to die! Then, when you're pale and shaking and paralyzed with panic, he says you're fine. And always adds as you walk out the door, "I wish *I* was in such good health."

Is there a doctor alive who isn't a specialist? And have you ever known *one* who wasn't "the top in his field"? Did you ever know anyone who didn't go to these *top* specialists? Have you ever heard anyone say, "I had a gallbladder condition, so I went to this mediocre doctor?"

My question is this: if everyone is going to these

top-notch specialists, how are all these schlepper doctors who nobody goes to making a living, and are they forced to play golf all day on mediocre courses?

If one of my own sons was going to be a doctor, I'd advise him to be a dermatologist. What could be better than dermatology? Kids will have acne until the end of time. Better yet, nobody calls a dermatologist in the middle of the night, and nobody dies from pimples.

Proctology . . . I say the jury still is out. I once had to see a proctologist and couldn't help asking him, "Does your mother know what you're doing for a living?"

Doctors terrify me, which is a tough way to be if you're also terrified of being sick. But even though I go in numbing panic, I try to maintain a sense of humor in the face of adversity. But there's adversity and there's adversity. And then there's gynecology.

If you're my age, you'd rather herd zebra than go to see your gynecologist. I've had one chuckle, in my entire life, during such a visit. It was back in New York, with an extremely popular gynecologist who had delivered my son a few months before.

I had gone to his office to ask a question. In detail I explained who I was, but the face of the busy doctor remained a blank.

"I'm sorry," he said, "but I really don't remember."

"You remember, you remember. I'm the lady who

had the little boy with the blue eyes."

"I still don't remember. I'm sorry."

He stared again at my face but could not place it.

"Get on the table," he said. "Then I'll remember."

Marcus Welby. Now there's a doctor.

I loved Marcus Welby. He went to patients' homes. He resurrected their entire lives. The great Marcus Welby would reunite couples. Mend broken dreams. Make deaf people hear and blind people see. My kind of doctor.

So were the doctors at St. Elsewhere (before they got canceled). When a patient had emotional problems, here came a St. Elsewhere doctor. Me, I've never had a doctor, not one, who gave a damn about my emotional problems. I never had a doctor call my husband or my sons, like they did on St. Elsewhere, and tell them how to treat me, how to love me, how to help me live my life totally devoid of stress and disease.

I've been sick in real life. Believe me, I'd rather be sick on TV.

My favorite strange-but-true doctor story involved a couple of our neighbors back in New York many years ago. Mrs. Schwartz got very ill, and her family decided to take her to this "big" doctor on Park Avenue.

The entire family went with her to the big-shot doctor. The doctor took all kinds of tests and instructed Mrs. Schwartz to return the following week. When Mrs. Schwartz went back to see the doctor, he sat her down to give her the distressing news.

"Mrs. Schwartz," he said, "I'm sorry to tell you, we're going to have to take out all your teeth."

"It's all right with me," Mrs. Schwartz replied.

At which point she reached in her mouth, took out her dentures, and placed them on the table.

So much for "big" doctors.

Do men get sick differently from women?

Of course. Women get sick. Men lose their minds.

At least that's how they make it seem. If there is a thankless, endless, hopeless task on this earth, it's having to cater to a male person who is sick. I have a husband, two sons, I have worked with hundreds of male actors, and I can't recall a single male who has ever gotten sick with the slightest shred of human dignity. If they don't feel better *immediately*, they regress to the maturity level of a 13-month-old child. They scream and cry and kick and make out their wills and mainline NyQuil. They are a large pain in the rear.

Now, if *I* should get sick, that's another matter. "It's just the flu," they say. "You'll be fine in the morning—and while you're up, could you make me a cheese sandwich?"

Some men like to wax heroic. "I'll do everything," they say. "Don't move an inch. I'll take care of everything."

So you lie down. You get a touch drowsy. Maybe you'll get a rest.

POUND.

It's him, slamming on your door.

"Come in," you gasp.

"Where do you keep the salt?"

"Do you have to light this stove, or does it go on by itself?"

"Those little bubbles. Does that mean the water is boiling?"

No more than I am, you think.

Whenever my husband wasn't feeling well, he would call Dr. Frankel. A sweet man, Dr. Frankel was no Ben Casey—he wasn't even Gentle Ben. Nor was he blessed with the sharpest eyesight. When he gave Arthur an injection, he would—no kidding—hold up the needle, and Arthur would kind of run into it with his arm.

A few years later, Dr. Frankel's asthma had gotten the best of him; he had given up medicine to become a shrink. Arthur and I were having some minor problems, and I wasn't exactly thrilled when he suggested we go to see Dr. Frankel.

It wasn't that I harbored any qualms about seeing a shrink. To the contrary, I have been seeing them for years and am a strong believer in the benefits of their gifts if you can find a good one. I think people should see shrinks not when they're facing a crisis, but when things are going well. *Everyone* has room for improvement, and *everyone* can use some self-illumination. I firmly believe in therapy, especially marital.

So no, it wasn't that. I just wasn't really sure about Dr. Frankel. But Arthur can be persuasive. So we went.

We went to his office, and as we took turns speaking, Dr. Frankel swung around his big leather chair so that he could gaze out the window. Unfortunately, he had also turned his back to us in the process, but I figured that was just his style.

So we went on talking, confiding in Dr. Frankel about the nature of our problem. Then, in midsentence, Arthur suddenly fell silent. We looked at each other, neither of us sure of what we were actually hearing. Yet it was unmistakable. Dr. Frankel was snoring.

As he presented an award to our show, Jimmy Stewart leaned toward me.

He said, "May I kiss you?"

I thought, *Kiss me? I'd drink your bathwater.*

9
Do Legends Go
to the Bathroom?

I used to watch a lot of movies when I was kid. I would daydream about the lives of the stars, people like Dorothy Lamour, Joan Crawford, Claudette Colbert, and Bette Davis. I'd picture them living in mansions laced with marble, with deep indoor pools and impossibly high ceilings that opened to the sky. At night, servants would undress them and draw their baths. After they'd bathed, servants would wait with those soft, luxurious robes.

I was sure that none of these legends ever went to the bathroom or, for that matter, did anything menial. A legend do the laundry?

Although that was many years ago, I don't think people have changed much. We still mythologize celebrities, especially in the United States where we have no royalty. We create our *own* royalty by turning entertainers and athletes into kings and queens.

I've been lucky enough to meet many of these people—even a few I used to daydream about—and I've made an incredible discovery: celebrities are just people. I know it sounds amazing, but I've learned to accept this truth.

So can someone please tell me: why, when I meet the giants of Hollywood, does my logic vanish, and I revert to that awestruck little girl?

I can't help it. When Bob Hope tells you you're a pistol, when Sammy Davis, Jr., says he's been trying to meet you, when Johnny Carson says he and his wife tape the show when they can't be home on Saturday nights, when you meet George Burns and Tony Randall and Danny Thomas and scores of wonderful people, you just stop dead in your tracks: "Holy moly! I don't think I believe this."

These people are warm and genuine; they make me feel so much like I belong. Yet I can't help thinking, *I'm not one of them, I'm one of us. I'm a fan.*

I remember the occasion when I shared a table with Jimmy Stewart. Outwardly I was being very cool. Inside I was oatmeal: *My God! I'm at the same table as Jimmy Stewart!*

Later in the evening, as he presented an award to our show, Jimmy Stewart leaned toward me.

He said, "May I kiss you?'"

I thought, *Kiss me? I'd drink your bathwater.*

I suppose the longer you're in the business, the more you acquire a sense of sophistication about these things. Apparently I'm running behind. I was at a big benefit one night, and a line of people was waiting for the valets to bring the cars. A hand reached out and touched my wrist, and before I turned I heard this warm, elegant voice: "Hi, how are you?"

I turned, and there was John Forsythe. I couldn't think of a damn thing to say.

I managed something like "Oh . . . I'm okay." Very original, very witty.

Of course, on my way home I was knockout clever. But I consoled myself with the knowledge, *John Forsythe knows who I am.*

At least I didn't do anything foolish, like jump up and down, as I did the time I met Pat Sajak.

First of all, I'm a game show nut. I watch even the bad ones, because I like to watch the people. I also like to see if I can compete. I just love game shows.

"Wheel of Fortune" is the best (I also love "Jeopardy!"). People don't call me during "Wheel of Fortune" because they know I don't take any calls. If my friends are over, and they're talking during "Wheel of Fortune," I tell them to clam up or leave.

One day Pat Sajak and I were doing a charity

event. There he was, standing five feet away. I literally began leaping up and down.

"Pat Sajak, Pat Sajak," I swooned. "Oh my God, there's Pat Sajak."

We met, I gushed, he was totally embarrassed. He was also wonderful. He even let me steal his name card from his dressing room door, and I put it in my house. I'll say it for print: I love Pat Sajak.

Mickey Rooney is another personal favorite; my interest in him goes *way* back. When I was a kid, I used to watch Mickey Rooney, this little bundle of talent, and I'd think if I ever went to Hollywood and met Mickey Rooney he would fall in love with me and marry me. We'd be the biggest, shortest stars in Hollywood. It was one of my major fantasies.

A couple of years ago, part of it came true when he played my boyfriend on the show. I was thinking, *Boy oh boy, after all these years I'm finally starring with Mickey Rooney.* What the heck? I figured. Why not tell him? So I revealed my childhood fantasy.

He said, "Wait, before we go any further, did I ever marry you?"

I said, "No, I'm one of the people you *didn't* marry."

I never married Garry Shandling either, but we did get very friendly when we did "Comic Relief." If you've seen his act or his TV show, you know that Garry's hair means the world to him. When Garry does his taxes, he claims his hair as a dependent.

During "Comic Relief," Garry told me he wanted

to go home for lunch but he didn't think he should jog.

"Why not?" I asked.

"Well, then I'll have to wash my hair again," Garry said.

"Why do you have to wash your hair again?"

"My hair is very important to me."

I laughed and went out to do my part of the show. I did a brief, emotional pitch about homeless kids who had to go out on the streets; it was one of the few serious spots on the show. When I went backstage I ran into Garry, who had been watching on the TV monitor.

"Boy, you were funny," he deadpanned. "We were broken up in here. We were hysterical, you were so funny."

Smart ass, I thought. "Oh yeah?"

"Yeah. That was a *real* funny speech."

"Thank you. . . . Incidentally," I said, smiling, "I hate your hair."

"Don't fool around."

"I'm not. I really hate your hair." I smiled some more.

"I'm very serious about my hair."

"I am too. I hate it."

Then I walked out of the room.

(Garry: I was only kidding. I love your hair. Really.)

When I read for the movie *Mask*, I was intrigued by the beautiful story. I was also thrilled by something else: a chance to work with Cher.

One afternoon on the set we were waiting to do a scene when I noticed that Cher looked upset. When I asked her what was wrong, she sighed and laid her head in my lap.

"I don't know what it is," she said. "I'm being a real bitch today."

That surprised me: if Cher was being a bitch, that day or any other, I didn't see it. All I saw was this perfectly gracious actress.

She began to ask me about myself and my kids and how long Arthur and I had been together. After I'd told her quite a bit, she started to tell me about herself.

"I was married twice," Cher said. "My first husband was much older than I, and we did this act together . . . and my second husband was a singer, and I was pregnant at the time, and he was already having drug problems. . . ."

As she went on I was thinking, *Cher, I read* People *magazine. I know when you wash your leotard.*

From that moment I loved Cher forever. She was so sweet and straightforward and ingenuous . . . I had told her about my life, now she was telling me about hers. She didn't tell me as though she was this luminous superstar. She told me as though she was just this girl and these were just things that had happened.

Cher's more than a wonderful actress. She's a lovely lady. I'm delighted to know her.

One of the great thrills of my life was meeting Cary Grant. It happened less than a month before he passed away. I was with my friend David at a testimonial for Abigail Van Buren, a lady I adore. David and I were checking out the guest list, and there it was . . . Cary Grant. I knew the guest list was awfully ritzy, but come on—Cary Grant?

David said, "He's sitting two tables away."

I nearly swallowed my shrimp fork. Then I slowly looked. There he was, Cary Grant, every bit as gorgeous and elegant as I had imagined.

Later Abigail came by our table. I never would have asked in a million years, but David said to her kindly, "You want to make Estelle's day? Her life? Introduce her to Cary Grant."

Abigail said, "Of course, darling, come with me."

I was thinking, *Really? You're not serious.*

She was serious.

As we walked over my heart was racing. I was taking these tiny steps like a little girl.

"Cary," Abigail said, "this is Estelle Getty from 'The Golden Girls.' "

I turned a bright shade of red, and Cary Grant stood up.

"I'm so pleased to meet you," he said. "I watch your show every opportunity I get. You're a very

funny lady. Give my regards to the rest of the ladies."

He smiled that smile, and I literally had to be
taken back to my seat.

Later on I saw Cary Grant get up. I asked David
where he was going.

"I don't know," David said. "Probably to the men's
room."

I said, "Follow him, follow him."

"Why?"

"I don't know. Just follow him."

David wouldn't do it, but it didn't matter. I was
floating.

People ask, "Have you had a hard time being chased around the casting couch?"

The answer is no. My body has taken the concept of the casting couch and turned it upside down. If I suspected I might not get a part, I'd threaten to get undressed.

10
Beyond the Chicken Suit: Adventures in Theater

My father wasn't an actor, but he should have been. People gravitated toward him—at family parties, they would literally gather at his feet. He told wonderful stories, did impersonations, spoke several languages and dialects. He never realized his talent.

My father inadvertently introduced me to the arts. I was four years old when he took the family across town to the Academy of Music, where we saw a movie and five acts of vaudeville.

I was stunned. I had found my world.

My life changed that day. Here I was, this little fat

girl living on the lower east side of New York. That day, I realized I belonged with those people up on the stage. So I invented myself. I became an actress in my heart and soul. And that's how it's been for my entire life.

When I was five, my father took me to a settlement house, where they held classes for children of immigrants, to help them absorb American culture. For 25 cents a week I had lessons in singing, dancing, and dramatics. I was on my way.

Understand this about actors: we're all a little crazy, and certainly in search of love. If we *weren't* in search of love, why would we do what we do? Why would we endure all the sweat and heartache? Why would we deal with all that rejection? Rejection is a part of any profession, but for an actor it cuts much deeper: they're not rejecting your product; they're rejecting you.

Why, then?

I assure you it's not for the money—most actors barely scrape by. I worked for many years for very little or nothing, yet I worked just as hard at my craft then as I do now.

Why, then?

The only true reward is this: a few minutes of love and applause from a group of anonymous people you'll probably never see again.

My sons say as long as writers keep creating parts

for mothers, I'll never have to look for a job.

I've played mothers throughout my career. I've played mothers to heroes and mothers to zeroes. I've played Irish mothers, Jewish mothers, Italian mothers, southern mothers, New England mothers, mothers in plays by Neil Simon and Arthur Miller and Tennessee Williams.

I've played mother to everyone but Attila the Hun.

I've also played mom to some very tall kids. There was Cher in *Mask*, Barry Manilow in *Copacabana*, Harvey Fierstein in *Torch Song Trilogy*, and now there's Bea in "The Golden Girls." I guess part of it is visual: paired with a tall kid, I'm a walking sight gag.

One time I thought I had a chance to be a mother in a Woody Allen movie. I was thrilled because I would kill to be in a Woody Allen movie. I would do more than that. I would work for free.

I went up for an audition for one of his films (I'd tell you the name, but I don't know what it is; I don't know if the movie was ever made.) When you read for Woody Allen, you're told not to talk directly to him; just cool it, don't ask questions, don't get intimate. So I just read the line.

It was Moses's mother talking to Jesus's mother.

Moses's mother says, "At least from the icons alone, you could make a living. But my son, nothing . . . I'm not saying he's stupid, he's not stupid. He's lazy."

That's all I recall about the script, but I do remember I came home and everyone thought it was the funniest thing they'd ever heard. (Mister Allen, if you're ever reading this book, I just want you to know that I'm not above a blatant plea: Use me! Please!)

I've been lucky. Even in plays that the critics mauled, my reviews were uniformly good. They weren't tributes to my performances, but to the words that were written on the page: no matter how obscure or esteemed the playwright, how horrid or inspired the play, the one part that is always written with heart and meaning and truth is the mother. It never fails.

Sometimes people are convinced I'm really the person I'm playing. When I played Mrs. Beckoff in *Torch Song*, women who had gay sons thought I really was Harvey Fierstein's mother. They would line up outside my dressing room to talk to me about their gay sons. They were absolutely amazed when I told them I wasn't Harvey's mother, nor did I have a gay son.

Even one of the kids connected with the show was confused.

"Are you the lady they found in Queens?" he asked.

"What do you mean?"

"Well, you're a regular person, aren't you? Didn't Harvey just kind of find you, and you fit the role?

You're not a real actress, are you?"

I said, "Give or take 30, 40 years, no."

That's show business—I've been at it forever, and there are still things I can't figure out. For instance, in most professions if you do something well, you get rewarded. If you do something well in show business, it can work against you.

I'm talking about typecasting. I did a play in New York called *The Divorce of Judy and Jane*, in which I played a lesbian. In that one year I must have gotten 12 offers to read for lesbian roles. Everything I'd done in my career up to that point was forgotten.

After *Torch Song*, every offer I got was for Jewish mothers from Miami. On "The Golden Girls" I play an Italian grandmother. Now that's all people think I can do.

Few people know this, but originally they wanted me to play Rambo. I said no. Didn't want to get typecast.

On the other hand, if you're going to be typecast, some roles are better than others. Once in New York I was sent to audition for an egg product commercial. Then I heard the bad news: you had to cluck like a chicken.

Clucking like a chicken was not my life's ambition, but neither was unemployment—I hadn't worked in five months. A little clucking wouldn't kill me.

When I arrived at the audition, there were many

other actors. I got up and did my chicken thing (for all you aspiring thespians, I prefer the Method chicken).

A few moments later I was told the job was mine. I was pleased.

"Now go next door," the director said, "and pick up your suit."

"What suit?" I asked.

"The chicken suit."

"The chicken suit?"

"Yes."

". . . I'm sorry."

"You're sorry? What do you mean, you're sorry?"

"I'm not taking the job."

"Why?"

"Because I won't wear a chicken suit."

"You said you haven't worked in five months."

"I haven't."

"You haven't worked in five months, and now you won't wear a chicken suit?"

"Right."

"You call yourself an actor?"

I wanted to laugh, but I didn't. I did hold firm, though. No way could I wear the chicken suit. What if I were good? I'd spend the rest of my life as a chicken?

I moved on and acted wherever I could: regional theater, summer stock, dinner theater, experimental theater, Kabuki theater, children's theater. I knew a lot of young, struggling writers, and I would perform their works all around New York, usually for free, just to get their plays mounted.

This path ended at some strange destinations. I once did a play called *Under the Bridge There's a Lonely Place with Gregory Peck and Me.* It had absolutely nothing to do with a bridge, a lonely place, or Gregory Peck, and none of us knew who "Me" was. No one could figure it out, including the critics, who savaged it. Since I played the only credible role, the mother, I was spared.

A reviewer wrote, "The play is nothing, and the only time it comes to life is when Estelle Getty rises above the material to make the mother a living, breathing person."

I went to the theater that night feeling pretty good about myself . . . until I encountered the rest of the cast.

"Wow," everyone was saying, "there she goes, rising above the material."

For sheer confusion, nothing tops a play I did in the late sixties. There were three characters: a guy in a dog suit, a son, and the mother. I was dressed in your basic motherly attire: a housecoat, rubber boots, and a whip.

It was a strange, weird, unintelligible play, but we did it anyway. Midway through the run, though, we realized we were lost; we had no idea where this thing was supposed to go. We called the playwright, and she agreed to come down to the city from upstate New York. She watched us do the play, and then the entire cast trooped over to her. We asked what she thought.

Noncommittally, she said she liked it.

"Well," I said, "we're glad you like it. But are we going in the right direction with it?"

Her eyes drooped to half-mast, and she took a long time to answer. I thought, *Good, here come the words of wisdom. Now we are going to learn what this avant-garde creation is really all about.*

"I'm going to be very honest with you," she said. "I'm sure I had something in mind when I wrote this, but now I don't have the vaguest idea what it was. I was a hippie back then. I was doing a lot of drugs."

Oh.

People ask me, "Just how far off Broadway did you used to work?"

Toilets. I worked toilets.

I once played in a storefront that held about 30 people. One rainy night there were more people onstage than in the seats. We had seven people in the cast and six in the audience. One of those six was a man with one arm, so he couldn't even applaud.

We did *Torch Song* once at a dance studio, in a circular arrangement so that seats were all around the stage. There was only one bathroom for cast and audience, and it was right near the stage. If someone had to use the bathroom during the show, the audience would be serenaded by a flushing toilet.

One night it rained like crazy right in on the stage. The actors, very cleverly and inconspicuously, kept shifting the plants so they'd catch the rain.

There was *always* some kind of physical hardship. I once shared a "dressing room" that was nothing more than some air space and a toilet. In this tiny space, a young man and I had to get dressed for the show together. We tried to stand back to back, but it was a chain toilet—every time we'd move, someone would get smacked in the head with the toilet chain.

In Philly I worked a house where they'd forgotten to build dressing rooms. When they realized their error, they built a little house *behind* the theater for the actors to dress in. The only way you could get there was to walk down a flight of stairs, across a long hallway, up a flight of stairs, and across another hallway. You had to be onstage half the time even if your cue wasn't up—you never knew how long it would take you to get back from the little house.

I've worked houses where you couldn't even go backstage—there *was* no backstage. If you had to exit a scene and enter later on the other side of the stage, you had to leave the theater, walk around the block, and come back in through the other entrance. I always imagined the day would come when the audience was awaiting my big entrance while I was in the alley getting mugged.

I'm not complaining: all of this is part of being an

actor. So is ad-libbing. It's part of your craft. You learn to ad-lib if you want to survive.

One night during *Torch Song* my character had made a box of cookies for her son, Arnold. Visiting from Miami, she was staying at his New York apartment.

"Mmmm, cookies," Arnold said.

I opened the box—a huge roach leaped out. I nearly had a stroke, but quickly recovered. I had to: the roach was so big, everyone in the audience had seen it.

"See?" I said. "This never happened when you were living with me."

In the play *Blithe Spirit*, I played Madame Arcati, a psychic. The hero, a handsome widower, is on the verge of remarriage. But the playful, deceased wife comes back to haunt her husband.

The "ghost" was supposed to appear when I said the line "Aha, I can smell her. I can feel her presence!"

But no ghost appeared. We ad-libbed for what was probably a full minute but seemed like several hours. Without tipping it off to the audience, we began to signal each other with our eyes, he eyeballing me, I eyeballing him, each saying with our eyes:

"You go offstage and get her. I'll stay here."

"No, *you* go offstage and get her. *I'll* stay here."

It was one of my most horrifying moments on stage. The play just ground to a halt.

Finally, when all hope had faded, she appeared.

The "husband" (her husband in real life) and I breathed a sigh of relief. We knew we'd get her later.

When the show was over and we were ready to leave, I asked Harve where his culprit wife Hedda was.

"She's locked herself in the bathroom and won't come out. She said she didn't mind facing me; the worst I could do was divorce her. But facing Estelle meant certain death."

One particular Mother's Day I was doing a play with a young man named Thom. Thom came racing up to my dressing room—there was a phone nearby.

"How long to my cue?" Thom asked me.

"About four minutes."

"Great. I want to call my mother and wish her a happy Mother's Day."

Thom rushed to the phone and dialed his mother long-distance.

"Hi, it's me, Thom."

Pause.

"Thomas."

Pause.

"Your *son*."

Pause.

"Your son *Thomas* . . . Right. Happy Mother's Day."

I was so convulsed I nearly fell down the stairs.

"I haven't been home in a long time," he explained. "A very long time."

Oh, an actor's life for me.

We had a lot of fun back then. We also got frustrated, but we never let it stop us. It was a simpler time, with no great expectations.

If I'm feeling especially sentimental, sometimes I can't help but wonder: wouldn't it be nice to go back to my roots, and work some of those same old toilets?

Naaaaah.

Believe it or not, I also used to be a stand-up comic.

Back then the business was radically different. Today female comics are hot. In my day they were as popular as public toe sucking. Today female comics can talk about sex. In my day they could also discuss sex, with a minor stipulation: they had to do it in Swahili.

Against the odds I tried it anyway, for two straight summers at a resort in the Catskills. I doubled as a busgirl in the children's dining room: first the kids would pelt me with Jell-O, then I'd get revenge by doing my act.

The only thing my routine lacked was humor. I think I knew this after that first summer, but I went back anyway. It was a great place to meet guys. All the waiters were studying to be dentists, and I always thought I'd wind up with a dentist. Not as good as an M.D., but what is?

After the Catskills, I tried my routine at some small clubs in New York. I still wasn't making it. Then I tried it on my friends. *They* pelted me with Jell-O.

For a woman, showbiz can be tough. People ask, "Have you had a hard time being chased around the casting couch?"

Once and for all, I'd like to set the record straight. The answer is no. Never. Not once. NO.

Nobody ever wanted to take me to bed. Nobody ever made a pass. My body has taken the concept of the casting couch and turned it upside down. If I suspected I might *not* get a part, I'd threaten to get undressed.

Relatively speaking, I'm not a superstitious person. I'm not saying I seek out black cats, but I don't let superstition rule my life.

The theater is another story. There, I abide by every rule. Everyone in theater knows what they are:

- Never wear green.
- Never whistle in a dressing room. If you do, you have to go outside, turn around three times, spit, and ask to be allowed back in.
- Backstage, never mention the name of that play written by Shakespeare about that king whose

name begins with M and has a second syllable that's a woman's name.

- Never wish anyone "Good luck." Instead, say "Break a leg" or *Merde*, which means shit in French.

I have a confirmed problem with limos. Maybe I'm too short to see above the crowd, or maybe I need new glasses—whatever, I can never find my driver. After an affair, it's time to go home, all the other guests find *their* drivers . . . and I discover my driver had hotter plans for the night. Within 10 minutes, the entire place has cleared out, and I'm standing on the curb by myself.

11
I Get Around:
A Saga of Lost Luggage

I've got bad luggage karma.

I should shave my head and hand out religious books—that's how much time I spend in airports looking for lost luggage. It defies explanation: in one brief period of time my bags got lost on four straight trips. I think that's a modern record.

I don't get it, because I do all the right things. I painstakingly fill out all the little name tags. I give handsome tips to the porters. I beg people to be careful. I refuse to move from the counter until I see my bags get on the trolley.

"Okay, is that going to the plane?" I ask.

The man says, "Don't worry, little lady. It's going to get on."

Then I go to Philly and my bags go to Burma.

When you've been burned more times than toast, you start to take precautions. Now if I'm flying somewhere, I'll put most of my stuff in two pieces of luggage, but I'll also carry on some evening clothes, makeup—all the stuff I'll need that night when they lose the other two pieces.

Carrying on all this stuff can break your back. So I put it all on my wheely thing. My wheely thing is one of those metal luggage carriers with the wheels and the elastic ropes . . . a wheely thing. I love it, but it's kind of awkward. Every time I try to stand it up straight it falls over, meaning I have to keep rearranging my bags, meaning I have to keep redoing the elastic ropes, meaning the people I travel with hate my wheely thing.

"Why don't you just carry your stuff or let me carry it?" they always grumble.

No way. You may lose my luggage, but you'll never get my wheely thing.

I also have a confirmed problem with limos. Granted, on the list of life's great hardships, losing your limo is not at the top of the list, yet the fact remains: limos and I are on different wavelengths. Maybe I'm too short to see above the crowd, or maybe I need new glasses—whatever, I can never find my driver. After an affair, it's time to go home, all the other guests find *their* drivers. Not me. My driver invariably has hotter plans for the night. Within 10 minutes, the entire place has cleared out, and I'm standing on the curb by myself.

The first time I rode in a limo that was sent exclusively for me, I thought it was marvelous. It was in California after I got the part on "The Golden Girls." I was attending my first network gala, and they said they'd send a limo. I told them it wasn't necessary. They told me not to worry, they sent a limo for everyone. I thought, *Boy, this is the height of luxury.*

The limo arrived, I strolled out nice and slow to where it was waiting . . . and no one was there to see me get in it. I felt like climbing on its roof and shouting, "Limo! Limo!"

My mother used to tell me, "It's easy to get used to good things. It's hard to go back." She was right. As I rode in that first limo I said to myself, "My God, what am I doing here?" The next time I rode in a *stretch* limo, which had a TV and a bar. The next time I had a stretch limo with a TV, a bar, and a telephone.

Now when I get a regular limo, I look around and think, What, no TV? No bar?

My friend, Rhoda, once asked me if I worried about terrorists when I flew on airplanes.

I said, "No . . . but I will now."

I'm petrified of flying. It doesn't even work for me as a concept: every time I get in the air I wonder how the hell we got this hunk of metal up here and how it's *staying* up here. If there's even a hint of turbulence, I'm like a kindergarten teacher—I want everyone to sit quietly in his seat. I figure it's safer that way.

I despise turbulence. The moment it starts, I descend into blind, abject fear. I'll look at the person next to me and think, *I'll do anything you want. Just save me when we start to go down and the oxygen mask falls out.* I also constantly watch the stewardesses to make sure they're still walking around and chatting. When stewardesses sit down I panic, because I know they've got to know something we don't.

I keep close tabs on the pilot too. When he strolls through the plane, I always have the impulse to say, "Okay, you've been out long enough. Now get back in there." Even if he's just going to the bathroom, I have to suppress the urge to ask, "Hey, did you tell your buddy to watch where he was going?"

I also scrutinize the people on the plane. Do they look like they're going to survive this? I always feel safer when the flight includes a baby. If there's a baby on the plane, I figure we'll be okay. I don't even mind if the baby cries a little.

Not all my fears are imagined. Like the time Arthur and I went to California for what we thought was some leisure and rest.

It was back in 1971: we were visiting cousins in

Los Angeles. Their three-bedroom home had a single bed in each bedroom; Arthur slept in one bedroom, and I slept in another.

At 3:00 A.M. I was startled from my sleep by a tremendous grinding sound, like a plane losing altitude and plummeting earthward. That was my first thought: *A plane is now going to land on our heads.* My second thought was, *My God, it's an atomic bomb.*

The house began to shake and rumble. A bookcase above my head broke, and the books came crashing down on top of me. I tried to get out of bed, but everything was shaking and I fell to the floor. Terrified, I started crawling for the door and calling for Arthur, who was trying to get to my room.

We all converged in the hall, and I started to cry.

"Oh my God," I shrieked "What is it?"

"It's an earthquake!" yelled my cousin.

And I thought, *Oh God. A thousand ways I've imagined I would die, earthquake never made the list.*

The next thought that entered my head was, *I know what everybody's going to say: "How like Estelle to die in an earthquake. She couldn't be mugged or die of a disease; she had to go in an earthquake."*

I was hysterical. And Arthur, cool as ice, had everything under control.

"Now listen, everybody!" he shouted. "Let's fill

up everything we can with water. I'll get the transistor radio."

Meanwhile the commode is flying across the room, and I'm thinking, How can he be so civilized?

"Are you all right?" Arthur whispered gently.

"I want to go home," I screamed. "Take me home!"

Well, we survived, along with the rest of the neighborhood. We were all evacuated to the beach, and we discovered later that not only was it one of the worst quakes in California history, but our cousins' home sat just a few miles from the epicenter.

I shouldn't have been surprised: Arthur and I always have problems when we travel together (although, thank God, we generally do not have to deal with earthquakes and flying toilets). Our most frequent ordeal: we never want to see the same things.

Arthur is intrigued by the technical things in life. In Europe he'll take me to lakes and explain to me for hours how they were formed. Or he'll take me to see turbines, and he'll say, "Do you realize all of this is concrete?"

I go because I know Arthur likes it, but I'm bored to death. When I'm in foreign countries, I like to do people-oriented things. I like to watch the kids in the streets, I like to check out the merchants and their little shops. I like obscure, nontouristy restaurants where I can stuff myself.

So we have this tolerance thing going. He does my stuff, I do his, and if we can't decide, we're democratic: we do what I want.

* * * * * *

I do a lot of benefits for various causes, and when I do, I always get put up at gorgeous hotels. When I arrive, there are always flowers and wine and fruit and lovely messages. The hotel people treat me marvelously.

A few years ago I did a benefit in Atlanta and the hotel's manager had sent flowers and fruit and a note to my room.

It said, "Welcome to the Ritz-Carlton, Buckhead."

I wasn't sure how to take that. "Buckhead"? I assumed it was a term of endearment in Georgia. At the same time, I'd never even met the man who wrote me the note, and I thought his calling me Buckhead was a little personal.

I wasn't going to mention it, but finally I was bested by my curiosity. I walked up to the man who was running the benefit.

"Why did they call me Buckhead?" I said. "Is that some kind of pet name around here?"

"Who called you Buckhead?" he said.

"The general manager in the note."

"The note?"

I showed him the note, and he broke into hysterics. He explained: in downtown Atlanta there are two Ritz-Carltons. The one I was staying at was in an area known as Buckhead. To differentiate, they called it the Ritz-Carlton, Buckhead.

The story spread like wildfire. Everyone at the hotel was calling everyone else Buckhead.

I received a great offer a couple of years ago: "Lifestyles of the Rich and Famous" asked me to go to Israel for one of its segments. I was delighted to have the opportunity, and had a wonderful, wonderful time.

For a few days I stayed on a kibbutz with the crew and my manager, Alan. It was lovely, very pure, but there wasn't a lot to do there. Even if you wanted to watch TV, there were only two channels, and one of them only showed the movie *Exodus*. I've been to Israel three times, and the only thing I've ever seen on that channel was *Exodus*.

So we're at this kibbutz, it's very serene, and Alan and I, a pair of New Yorkers, contract intense cabin fever. We decide to go see a slide show on the history of the kibbutz. We stroll through magnificent grounds, up a flight of stairs, through a hallway, down a flight of stairs, and through another hallway—to discover an empty room. There is a slide projector and a screen, the seats are all arranged in four neat sections, but no people.

The kibbutz was usually quiet, but this is *silence*. Alan goes to the first section and sits down. I take a seat in the middle section. I have no idea why, but for the next 20 minutes we sit in this room, alone, completely silent, and stare at a blank white screen. Finally, we glance at one another . . . and become absolutely hysterical. Tears, aching stomachs—can't stop.

Four people finally struggled in, and we had to compose ourselves. The six of us watched some old slides of the kibbutz, applauded, and left. The moment we were alone, Alan and I cracked up again. All through Israel, every time we mentioned the slide show, we'd become hysterical.

See what peace and quiet can do to you?

I once went to Vegas with my sister Roz. I joined the trip late, so she was already rooming with another woman, Carmela. When I arrived, I went to see Roz in her room, and noticed both she and Carmela had already unpacked, except for a valise that was standing erect in the middle of the room. I knew it wasn't Roz's, but neither she nor I said a word: if Carmela wanted to keep her valise standing upright in the middle of the room, that was her business, even though everyone else had to keep stepping over it.

We had dinner that night with an organization of women, and everyone, except for one lady, was all dressed up. This poor woman was wearing Bermuda shorts, a cotton shirt, socks, and a pair of sneakers. She didn't look too happy.

The next night we saw the sad lady in the same pair of Bermuda shorts again. She shrugged and explained that the airport had lost her luggage. These were all the clothes she had.

At the end of the weekend, I went to Roz's room so we could check out, stepping carefully over Carmela's valise, which was still standing upright in the middle of the room.

"You better tell Carmela to take her valise," I whispered to Roz.

Roz said, "Carmela, don't forget this valise."

Carmela just looked at her. "It's not my valise. It's yours."

"No, it's not. I took my valise away."

"So did I."

Roz looked at Carmela. Carmela looked at Roz. They said it at the exact same time: "You mean that's not your valise?"

It didn't belong to either of them! We had a good laugh, then we went downstairs to check out, where we told the man at the desk about the mysterious valise. His face went pale.

"Oh no!" he said, "That fits the description of the bag belonging to the woman who lost her luggage."

The poor lady in the Bermuda shorts had to wear the same clothes for three days because Roz and Carmela were both too polite to say, "Please get your lousy valise out of the middle of the room."

My best acting was not conducted on any stage. It happened with Roz. *Quelle aventure!*

Let me set the scene. Roz and I were going to

cruise the Greek Islands. We got dropped off at the New York airport, and we couldn't wait. We got in the ticket line, checked our bags, pulled out our passports—and discovered that Roz had picked up the wrong one. The canceled one.

We were traveling with a group of people as part of a tour, so we couldn't change our reservations. The plane was leaving in 30 minutes, we were 35 minutes from home, no car. Our great trip was slipping away, and we were frantic.

I got an idea. It was risky, it was a longshot, it was daring. In other words, it wasn't me.

On the other hand, the Greek Islands . . .

I sprung into action.

I took out my passport, put Roz's passport beneath it, and handed them both to the attendant for stamping. The attendant stamped mine, and as he picked up Roz's, a split second before he could look at it I gave him a sharp poke in the shoulder.

"Please," I blurted, "where do I go to get Greek drachmas?"

"Just a minute," he said. "I'll be right with you."

I never stopped talking: "We're going to Greece, but we don't have Greek money. What do we do? How can we tip the driver? We don't have Greek money. Can I change it now? What do we do?"

He kept looking down, trying to check the passport, but every time I'd ask a question he'd look back up. In the confusion he stamped Roz's passport.

We were on the plane to Greece.

Well, I did the same thing for two entire weeks—the layered passports, the poke, the onslaught of questions. We did it at every hotel, every port—we even got money out of banks. Not one person noticed that the passport wasn't good.

That first time at the New York airport, my heart had been hammering so hard I nearly collapsed. I was sure what I was doing was so illegal they'd not only keep us off the plane, they'd throw us in prison. By the end of the trip I was feeling downright bold. It got to the point where people on our tour were following us to the bank to see me do it.

I got my sister through all of Greece with a canceled passport. It was some of the finest acting of my life.

My friends in New York are the only people in the world who like to eat as much as I do. When I'm with them, I find myself walking around like one of those kids in a snowsuit, my arms stuck out at my sides. I always wish I was wearing a belt so I could unbuckle it.

12
My Fabulous Friends

When I won the part of Sophia, my friends were delighted with my success. Loyal New Yorkers, they were also certain I'd never survive in Los Angeles.

"You'll never make it out in Hollywood," they warned. "You'll never find anyone to be friends with; you won't find anyone to talk to. You're a real New York person."

After a month in California I received a phone call from one of my friends back east. He wanted to know how I could possibly be surviving.

"Well," I said, "it's one of two things. Either I've

met the most interesting, most entertaining, brightest people in Hollywood, or else I'm incredibly shallow. I must tell you, I'm having a ball."

I am having a ball. The people I've met in Hollywood are funny and smart and loving and supportive. I have friends like that in New York, and now I've got them here.

If I have a talent for anything in this world, it's a talent for people. I've been lucky enough to have as friends some of the most wonderful people in the world . . . and also the most colorful.

For instance, one of my friends (who shall remain nameless) is very attractive and used to live this great carnal life. She was this untamed creature doing things the rest of us never did—I've never seen so many people live vicariously off of one person.

She was once having an affair with a married man. He was hopelessly enamored and constantly spoke of making their relationship more deeply committed. One late afternoon in their motel room, in a great romantic moment, he took her in his arms.

"I'll leave Sharon," he cooed. "We'll go to Mexico and start a new life together."

Then he paused. "Wait a minute. Is this Thursday?"

"Yes," she answered.

"Oh no," he gasped. "I have to get home! Tonight I do the weekly shopping, and the A&P gets crowded early!"

Another time I received a frantic early-morning phone call.

"Prince Street . . . what borough is it in?" she asked.

"How should I know?" I said. "Why?"

"Well"—she hesitated—"I met this man last night, and we went back to his place, which is where I am now, but it was dark when we came here, and he left early this morning, so now I don't know where I am."

Why did I even ask?

She continued. "I'm looking out the window . . . I see a bakery and a phone booth and a pet store and lots of telephone wires. . . ."

"Brooklyn," I said. "It's got to be Brooklyn. Go to the subway and take the—"

"Don't bother," she interjected. "I'll grab a cab and meet you for lunch."

"A CAB?" I screamed. "It'll cost you a *fortune!*"

"Estelle," she said, "*whatever* it costs . . . it was worth every penny."

Another friend of mine, Betty, is one of the funniest people on earth. She used to work as a psychiatric nurse, and she absolutely hated her job. She did, however, love to eat, and once the combination got her in trouble.

One day Betty was distributing meal trays to the patients, and she got hungry (which shows how much she loved to eat, if she could get hungry looking at hospital food). When no one was watching, she ate one of the patient's chocolate puddings before she served the tray. Then Betty gave the woman the tray, and when she came back later to pick it up, the woman asked Betty why she hadn't gotten her chocolate pudding.

"You did get it," Betty said. "You ate it already."

I asked her how she could do that to a patient. Betty said the woman deserved it—she was cruel and consistently abusive. This same woman, incidentally, thought she was Joan of Arc and was always telling Betty that she was terrified of fire.

"So what did you tell her?" I asked Betty.

"I said I didn't blame her," Betty said. "I told her she was Joan of Arc. She *should* be afraid of fire."

I love Betty. I love all my friends in New York, and I miss them. I see them every time I go back—but it's not enough. With great old friends, is it ever?

I miss Rhoda, whom I can look at and say, "Rhoda, now I'm going to wiggle my finger and make you laugh," then I wiggle my finger, and she'll laugh.

I miss Sylvia Z., who doesn't think she's good-looking. She says it's true that beautiful women spend Saturday nights alone, because every Saturday night of *her* entire youth, she had a date.

I miss Sylvia A., who talks more than I do; Pearl, who thinks I could still be playing ingenues ("A little powder, a little rouge, you'd be fine"); and Charlotte, whom I can talk to 10 times a day about everyone and everything.

I miss *all* my great friends in New York, people

I've known and loved for 30 or 40 years. I miss the laughs and even the tears.

I also miss the eating.

My friends in New York are the only people in the world who like to eat as much as I do. When I'm with them, I find myself walking around like one of those kids in a snowsuit, my arms stuck out at my sides. I always wish I was wearing a belt so I could unbuckle it.

When I'm back home, we don't even give directions like most people do. For us, street names are irrelevant:

"There's a small Italian restaurant on the corner—I think it's called Alfredo's—take a left and go two blocks. At the A&P—check that, it's a Safeway—make another left. Turn right at Carvel, left at Dunkin' Donuts, go straight until you hit the little kosher deli with the great corned beef. I'll meet you there."

Hey, girls, see you soon. Save me a piece of cheesecake.

Most of my friends in New York are my age. Many of my friends in California are also my age—divided by two.

We have a lot of fun, we like the same things. We constantly talk about theater, we go to plays, movies, comedy clubs . . . we just hang out. I love their *joie de vivre*.

I didn't purposely seek younger friends when I

moved to California; that's just how it worked out. I never gave it much thought, until one day when I was sitting in a room with about 10 friends and it struck me: everybody in that room was young enough to be my child.

What did I do when I made this shocking discovery? What was I supposed to do? Bolt out of my chair? Scream at them as I fled the room, "Goddamn it! You people couldn't care *less* about Preparation H!"

Friendship isn't about age. It's about friendship.

People say to me, "Do you mother these kids?" No, I don't. I like to give them comfort, but I like to comfort older people too. I never, ever think of myself as the mother of these kids. They've all got their own mothers, and one mother is enough. Besides, I've got two kids of my own, and they're enough, too.

I cherish my younger friends. When I did *Torch Song Trilogy*, I was the only older person in the play, and I think it's a period of time that none of us will ever forget. When we were doing the show in California, every Sunday before our matinee I'd cook brunch for the entire cast. Since the show had three acts, everyone had to go to the theater at a different time, so it wasn't your typical brunch. First I'd make something early for my roommate, David . . . then later a few more actors would file in . . . a few more after that . . . and so on. By the time *I* had to go to work, I'd cooked five breakfasts—and eaten four of them.

I loved it—those kids took good care of me. Yet they never looked at me as an "old person," never treated me with any more or less decorum than they would a friend their own age. Oh, they might offer me the softer chair. Otherwise, they were perfectly happy to run me ragged.

Take Donald, for instance, one of the brilliant young actors from *Torch Song*. For a while he stayed with me, and what started as a few days stretched into an extended visit. The thing about Donald is, he doesn't live with you—he lives all over you.

Donald is also a writer, which isn't hard to tell—he leaves a trail of paper everywhere he goes. He also loves to sleep late, while I'm Miss Up-and-At-'Em. On days when the maid came, I'd nag him before he could open his eyes: "Wake up! Clean up your mess! The maid is coming!"

When I really nagged him good, there was only one way Donald could stop me.

"Estelle," he'd say, "I'm one minute away from a pill. You better stop. I'm one minute away from a Valium." Only then would I take pity.

Or he'd addresss me as Miss Honeymouth, which always cracked me up.

Finally, near the end of his "visit," Donald asked me if he'd overstayed his welcome.

"Yes," I screamed, "more than overstayed your welcome. Get a ticket and go back to New York. Tonight if possible."

"In other words . . ." he said.

"Not in other words, in those exact words," I said.

Then I cried when he left.

Then there's David, another young actor and a former roommate. The perfect roommate. He's tall—he could reach things for me in the cabinets. He's got a good sense of direction—if I have to make more than three turns, forget it. He fixes things— I'm the least mechanical person in the world. Mechanical things give me brain lock. I can turn on my self-cleaning oven, but I can't get it to clean, because I don't know how. I don't know how to change my clocks or program my VCR. The only thing I can use my microwave for is to boil water. If I get my refrigerator open, I walk around the house feeling pretty jaunty.

I had it good with David.

He had it pretty good, too. In return for his reaching and fixing and driving, I would do the cooking and cleaning and shopping. Actually, by the time David moved out, he knew how to cook two different things (not well, but you can't have everything).

As roommates, David and I gave new meaning to the word *glamour*. Our idea of a big night out was the Sizzler and a movie, passing out in front of the

TV, and both of us waking up and yelling at each other to go to sleep.

As I said before, David's tombstone will read, *Here lies J. David Krassner. Estelle Was Right.* He says mine will read, *Here Lies Estelle. Where's David?*

Which is probably right, because I need him and love him a lot. I hope he never moves too far away.

The great thing about friends, real friends, is that you can agree to disagree. So what if you don't see eye to eye? It's part of life, and friends accept that.

What irritates me is when people disagree, and rather than accept it, they cop out: they say, "we're not communicating."

I think *communication* is one of the most misused words in our language. This is what I mean:

Very often during discussions and arguments when things are really getting hot, someone invariably says "You don't understand—we're not communicating." What he *means* is, "If you understood what I was saying, you'd agree with me."

When people tell me we're "not communicating," I say, "I hear what you're saying. I understand what you're saying. I just don't agree with you. Can you handle that?"

Another thing that drives me crazy is self-centered people. We all know them: people who see everything in this world, good or bad, only in relation to themselves.

The first time a man went to the moon, I turned to a friend and said, "My God, what a feat."

She said, "I would never do it. Not I. I would *never* do something like that."

I said, "Who asked you?" I couldn't believe what I was hearing. She even saw going to the moon in terms of herself.

Torch Song Trilogy changed the face of American theater. It was the height of daring: Harvey Fierstein wrote a play about gay people, a human interest story that could have been about anybody. I played a mother who learns to accept her son's gay lifestyle, and in the process I became very involved with the gay community. It was as if I'd become the quintessential mother of gays. Gay men and women who saw the play felt I understood their lifestyle. And I did.

I have many gay friends. We have talked at great length and in depth about homosexuality, and to anyone who thinks that being gay is a choice, I want to go on record as saying that they couldn't be more wrong.

No one wakes up one morning, at age 12 or 19 or 30, looks in the mirror, and says, "Yes, I think I'll be gay." Just as no one *decides* to be straight. No one chooses his or her sexual proclivity—people are what they are. Ten percent of every population in the world is homosexual, and no man-made laws can change that. There are too many people in this world who try to dictate what is right and what is wrong. You can't dictate feelings. Please, live and let live.

For me, all relationships must be based on honesty. I don't mean honesty to a fault. You don't say to someone, "Boy, have you gotten fat, and you should never wear purple, because it doesn't match the red in your eyes."

A good friend though, is someone who does more than give praise. A good friend doesn't fudge when you ask a difficult question. Sometimes it's our *best* friends who have to tell us when we're being jerks.

My sister once said to me, "You can get away with it." This is only partly true—with *friends* I can get away with anything. I can say terrible things, and people don't get hurt. I guess that's because I say it with humor instead of hostility.

David once asked me if I liked his new coat.

"Of course," I said. "I loved it when it was in style, and I love it now."

He knew I didn't like the coat, but he wasn't hurt, because I made him laugh. Anyway, David makes up his mind for himself—it's quite possible he really didn't care whether I liked his coat.

It all comes down to knowing your friends, who can take a joke and who can't. If I've got a friend who's lost her job and her marriage is rocky and she's gained 20 pounds, I don't say, "Guess what? Your earrings are ugly, too."

But I may just buy her a new pair.

A Last Word ... or Two

G ee, I guess this is it. The end of the book. I was just getting warmed up.

Oh well, the end of the book is the end of the book: time to say good-bye, to tell you I've had fun. Time to say thank you.

The end of a book is often something else: a place where many authors, in one guise or another, get philosophical—where they ponder the secret of life. If it's good enough for established authors, it's more than good enough for me.

The secret of life, huh? You sure you don't want my recipe for mushroom barley soup? I'm telling you, it's dynamite.

Okay, okay. Here, in the form of a story I once heard, is my final word on the secret of life:

There once was a young man who went on a quest for knowledge. He traveled to India, to the top of its highest mountain. At the very peak lived the fabled Guru of Gurus.

The man climbed days and nights, for many months. He took shelter in caves and subsisted on berries. Finally he reached the top of the mountain. There was the Guru of Gurus.

The man said, "Tell me, Guru, what is the secret of life?"

The Guru, after a long and profound silence, said, "Life is a fountain."

The man was astonished. "I've traveled for months, I've risked my life to find you—now you tell me life is a fountain?"

And the Guru said, "It's not?"

I wish you all a fountain of love and laughter.